TALES FROM RED VIENNA

by David Grimm

TALES FROM RED VIENNA
Copyright © 2022 David Grimm
ALL RIGHTS RESERVED

COPYRIGHT NOTICE: This Play is fully protected under the copyright laws of the United States of America and all countries covered by the International Copyright Union (including the British Commonwealth, Canada, Australia), the Berne Convention, the Pan-American Copyright Convention, and the Universal Copyright Convention, as well as all countries throughout the world with which the United States has reciprocal copyright relations. All rights, including but not limited to professional, amateur, and educational stage rights, motion picture, recitation, lecturing, public reading, radio broadcasting, television, video, YouTube, Zoom or any such Internet service or transmission, or sound recording, all other forms of mechanical or electronic reproduction, such as CD-ROM, CD-I, DVD, information storage and retrieval systems and photocopying, and the rights of translation into foreign languages, are strictly reserved. No part of this book may be reproduced, or transmitted in any form, by any means, now known or yet to be invented, without the prior written permission of TRW Plays in its capacity as publisher.

PERFORMANCE WARNING and ADVISORY: Professional, amateur, and educational groups are hereby advised that performance of this Play requires a license and is subject to payment of a royalty whether or not admission is charged. The stage performance rights throughout the world for this Play are controlled exclusively by TRW Plays. No professional, amateur, or educational performance may be given without obtaining, in advance of any and all performances, the written permission of TRW Plays and paying the requisite fee. Current royalty rates and performance information may be found at our website at www.trwplays.com and www.trwplays.co.uk. Inquiries concerning all other rights should be forwarded on to

TRW Plays
A division of Theatrical Rights Worldwide
1180 Avenue of the Americas, 6th Floor
New York, NY 10036
trwplays@theatricalrights.com

and

TRW Plays
A division of Theatrical Rights Worldwide
122-124 Regent Street
London W1B 5SA UK
trwplays@theatricalrights.co.uk

TRW Plays ATTRIBUTION: Professional, amateur, and educational licensees shall include the following notice in all programs, advertisements, and other printed material distributed or published in connection with the production of the Play:

TALES FROM RED VIENNA
is produced by special arrangement with TRW Plays.
www.trwplays.com
www.trwplays.co.uk

Printed in the U.S.A. / U.K.
ISBN: 978-1-63852-125-9

TALES FROM RED VIENNA was commissioned by the Huntington Theatre Company (Peter Dubois, Artistic Director, Michael Masso, Managing Director) through the Stanford Calderwood Fund for New American Plays; The play was workshopped at JAW: A Playwrights Festival produced by Portland Center Stage; subsequently, an edited version was produced by Manhattan Theatre Club, NYC (Lynne Meadow, Artistic Director, Barry Grove, Executive Producer) with funds provided by an Edgerton Foundation New American Play Award, on February 26, 2014.

Acknowledgments

Special thanks to Lisa Timmel, Robert Egan, Kelly Miller, Melinda Paige Hamilton, Rose Riordan, Chris Coleman, David Esbjornson, Braden Abraham, Mandy Greenfield, Anita Yavich, Kathy Chalfant, and Tina Benko.

Synopsis

Set as an enormous political tide is turning throughout Europe, *Tales from Red Vienna* explores the effects of war on women, the circumstances that control their lives, and the dreams that set them free.

Character List

HELÉNA ALTMAN *(W)*
EDDA SCHMIDT *(W)*
RUDY ZUCKERMEYER *(M)*
"MUTZI" VON FESSENDORF *(W)*
BÉLA HOYOS *(M)*
KARL HUPKA *(M)*

Setting

1920. Heléna Altman's apartments in the Mariahilf District of Vienna, and in the Zentralfriedhof Cemetery.

Run Time

Two hours.

"There are tragic elements in superficial things
and silliness in the tragic.
There is something suffocatingly sinister in what we call Pleasure.
There is lyricism in the dress
of a prostitute and something common-
place about the emotions of a
lyric poet.
No one thing can be excluded,
none considered too
insignificant to become
a very great power...
Everything is part of the dance...
In the words of the poet Jala-ud-din Rumi,
he who knows the power of the dance does not fear Death,
for he knows that Love kills."

—Hugo von Hofmannstahl

SCENE ONE

Night. The ticking of the clock. A key in a lock.

HELÉNA enters, leaving the door ajar. She's dressed in full mourning: black coat, black dress, hat, veil, gloves. She removes her coat and stands uncertain.

A MAN appears in the doorway. He is something of a dandy, but exudes a certain seediness. He's cold. HELÉNA lights a small lamp and removes her hat and veil. She can't bring herself to look at him directly. The MAN removes his coat and puts it, his hat, and gloves on the table and takes in his surroundings.

There is an awkward moment of inaction.

MAN:
So...

He steps up to her amorously and reaches for her. She draws his attention to a small silver tray.

He produces a billfold and places two notes on the tray. HELÉNA is immovable. The MAN places a third note on the tray. Still without looking at him, she removes her

ACT ONE

The front room of Heléna Altman's apartment in the Mariahilf District of Vienna.

Near the front door is a large table. There is a cabinet for dishes and wine and liquor glasses. A sitting room area. A window, decorated with heavy curtains. A tiled coal stove. An arched hallway which can be curtained off leads to the kitchen. A short hall leads to the bedroom door. The furnishings — Biedermeier and later periods — don't quite belong in the space. They came from the larger, nicer home Heléna lost. Clearly, much has been sold and we have reached the basics.

gloves.

He removes his jacket excitedly. He begins undoing her dress. Clumsily.

MAN:
(Humorously frustrated by her dress) These —

HELÉNA:
(Wishing him to remain silent) Please.

Silenced, the MAN proceeds in trying to undo her dress. His frustration grows and once or twice he grows forceful, almost violent. He takes a deep breath to calm down.

Growing weary of the dress, he hikes her skirts up against a table. He enters her suddenly. She is about to cry out but covers her mouth with her hand.

He fucks her. HELÉNA doesn't cry.

He tries to kiss her, but she keeps her head away. He is very excited by her and climaxes, burying his face in her clothes.

A moment of spent breathing.

He withdraws and turns his back, shyly buttoning himself up. Now it is he who has trouble looking at her directly.

He verbalizes a sound, part sigh, part nothing in particular, but it helps him regain himself. He puts on his jacket and checks himself in a wall mirror. The sex having pleased him, he whistles a tune to himself from Beethoven's Sixth Symphony. Hurt and horrified by his whistling, HELÉNA watches him as he puts on his overcoat.

He goes to her and reaches to touch her.

MAN:
Could we —

She pulls away as though stung.

Perplexed and disconcerted by her response, he withdraws. He takes up his hat and gloves and goes to the door. Turns, looks at her. She won't look at him. He exits.

HELÉNA grabs the money on the tray.

SCENE TWO

Several weeks later. Late morning. A very bright and cold day.

RUDY is unpacking groceries from his delivery box onto the large table. EDDA goes back and forth from the table to the kitchen, putting the groceries away. From upstairs, the sound of a bad beginner violinist practicing Adele's Laughing Song from "Die Fledermaus".

RUDY:
Frauline Edda, I can —

EDDA:
Every time I look at you, Rudy, you're more like your father. Not as he is today. I don't mean that drunken mess of a man. When he was younger. Quite a looker, he was. For a greengrocer.

RUDY:
(noticing an envelope under the door; putting it on the table) I can bring the box into the kitchen. It could save time.

The music upstairs stops in mid-phrase.

EDDA:
What are these? I didn't order cut flowers.

RUDY:
They're for Heléna. It's her birthday.

EDDA:
"Heléna"? She's Frau Altman to you, little rabbit.

> *The violinist upstairs starts over from the beginning.*

Yes, I know the story: when you were three years old, she took your face in her hands down among the radishes and told you to call her Heléna. He's been in love with her ever since.

RUDY:
Won't she like them? Doesn't she like white roses?

EDDA:
It's cut flowers she doesn't care for. Says when you give cut flowers, you've giving a dead thing. Still, nice to brighten up the room.

RUDY:
Give them back.

EDDA:
She'll appreciate the sentiment.

RUDY:
I'll bring her live flowers. Bulbs. A plant.

EDDA:
Rudy, you're eighteen. Go chase a girl your own age.

> *He doesn't budge. EDDA sighs and hands him back the flowers.*

What are you going to do? Throw them out? Roses in a rubbish heap is a sorry sight.

RUDY:

That's what you do with dead things. Just ask the Kaiser.

EDDA:

Listen to him: "Ask the Kaiser" — is that what your father says?

RUDY:

My father says we lost the war because we let the Kaiser down. *(An imitation)* "There was no morale!" I could have fought, you know —

> *Again, the violinist upstairs stops in mid-phrase.*

I should have run away when I was sixteen. You wouldn't be treating me like a child. Who knows but I would have ended up in Flanders fighting alongside Captain Altman. Maybe I would have saved his life.

EDDA:

Maybe you would have gotten yourself killed like he did and then how would you feel? It's a lucky thing they kicked the Kaiser in the backside before you were old enough to get yourself hurt.

RUDY:

My father says if the war had lasted another two weeks, we would have won.

EDDA:

And after those two weeks, it would have been another two weeks, and another, and another, like a gambler who can't stop himself. Any war that starts with flag-waving and parades doesn't end well. One should never mix alcohol and patriotism. *(Picking up the envelope)* What's this?

RUDY:

It was under the door.

> *The violinist upstairs continues. EDDA opens the envelope and reads. Frowns. Puts it away.*

What is it?

EDDA:

Did you manage to find any cream?

RUDY:

Here. And a bag of real coffee (that's a gift from me).

EDDA:

Where on earth — ? *(Smelling the coffee)* Don't tell me. Just promise me you're careful. *(Exiting into kitchen)* I'll pay for this with my own money.

RUDY:

I said, the coffee's a gift! You never listen. *(Pause.)* I don't like these apartments. Doesn't she feel cramped after living in such a big house? Sometimes when I'm coming from the shop, I still forget and go right on Gumpendorfer instead of left. All the doors had glass doorknobs, remember?

EDDA:

(re-entering, re: violinist) Someone should cut that child's hands off at the wrist.

> *EDDA pays RUDY as HELÉNA enters, still in*

mourning, unpinning a cameo from her dress.

HELÉNA:
Edda, I want you to go up and ask that child to forgo playing this afternoon, at least while Mutzi's here. Good morning, Rudy. How's your father? *(To Edda)* And don't forget the silver sugar bowl. And put some coal on so it's warm when she gets here. It's cold as a crypt.

EDDA starts putting coal in the stove and lighting a fire.

I'm having an old friend over for coffee, Rudy. What do you think — *(She holds up a pearl brooch and the cameo alternatively)* Pearl? Cameo?

EDDA:
Cameo and don't ask the boy questions he can't answer. Anyway, he was just going. Good-bye, Rudy.

HELÉNA:
Edda, let the boy speak.

RUDY:
I like the pearl. But then I'd like anything you chose.

Upstairs, the violinist stops mid-phrase.

Happy birthday. I have a gift for you but I'll have to come back to deliver it.

HELÉNA:
Rudy, you needn't bother with a gift.

RUDY:
It's never a bother when it's you. I'll be right back... Heléna.

RUDY exits. EDDA and HELÉNA laugh.

EDDA:

He's in love with you. It's hopeless.

HELÉNA:

(pinning on pearl brooch) Rudy's kind, that's all. Natures of his sort aren't all that common anymore. You shouldn't shame him.

EDDA:

I wasn't shaming him. I don't shame people. Shame on you. *(Producing the envelope from her pocket.)* This was under the door.

HELÉNA:

I suppose it opened itself? *(Reading it)* This is a mistake. It must be. *(Pause.)* Only put on enough coal to cut the chill. And see if you can cover that bit of the carpet; it's starting to fray. Oh Edda, why must she come today of all days? Women can be the vilest friends when they remember your birthday.

EDDA:

I can hear her now — *(an imitation)* "Heléna, darling! Would you look at yourself!" *(Moving furniture to cover the spot of fraying carpet)* That woman and her human ham hock of a husband. To them, the war was simply something that happened to other people.

HELÉNA:

(At mirror) Look at myself indeed. Then again, a widow is supposed to look a touch haggard, otherwise no one trusts her. My neck is still good, though.

EDDA:

(looking at herself in the mirror next to her) It's a perfectly lovely face. *(Indicating her own)* Be grateful you didn't get one of these.

HELÉNA:

What are you talking about? I love your face.

EDDA:

I'm what a widow is supposed to look like. Two eyes stuck in a burlap sack. You're still a young woman. You've got your health.

HELÉNA:

(looking at the mirror) Did you know Jews cover their mirrors when they're in mourning? It's so their thoughts remain on the departed, not on themselves. I was thinking about Rudy. When his mother was taken by influenza and that lovely mirror by the front door of their shop — you know the one — they had it covered in a sheet. Actually, I think it's so they won't have to see that level of pain in their own eyes. Grief is a disease... All right, that's it! I want Time to stop. I have experienced everything I care to. From here on in, time should move backwards.

EDDA:

(has opened a locked cabinet and taken out and poured a glass of schnapps) I'm pouring you a short glass. Won't do you any harm. Just take it.

HELÉNA:

(nervously) Now don't forget that child upstairs. I'm sure Mutzi suspects I'm living in squalor. I don't need Paganini to confirm it.

EDDA:
Drink.

> *EDDA holds out a glass. HELÉNA shakes her head. EDDA shrugs and knocks back the drink.*

HELÉNA:
Why is it so wrong to want to shut one's door to the world? What is it that's so wonderful out there?

> *The doorbell. They look toward the door but neither woman moves.*

She was always punctual. *(Almost a whisper)* Give me one of those.

> *EDDA pours a glass of schnapps. HELÉNA downs it, smells her breath. EDDA produces a small bottle of eau de cologne from her pocket. HELÉNA quickly dabs her cheeks.*

EDDA:
Are we ready?

> *HELÉNA seats herself. Breathes. Nods. EDDA answers the door. MUTZI von FESSENDORF.*

Countess von Fessendorf.

MUTZI:
Dear God, Edda, are you still with us? *(Handing wrap and gloves)* Incidentally, it's plain Frau Fessendorf now. Those charmless Communists with their abolition of nobility will reduce all human pleasure to a bodily function. They've given us women the vote (which I can't be bothered with), but taken away our titles (and honestly, whom does it hurt?)

Leave it to them and we'll all end up looking like boiled potatoes. Heléna darling, would you look at yourself!

HELÉNA:

Mutzi!

MUTZI:

No, don't *(kisses her cheek)* get up *(kisses other cheek)* — isn't this weather wretched? I want to murder my driver. Look at that: you're wearing your hair differently —

HELÉNA:

Yes, I —

MUTZI:

I don't like it. I'm joking! *(She laughs.)* No, it's so much simpler. *(Kisses her again.)* Happy birthday, my sweet Heléna, and many, many happy returns. Where is it? I had something. For you. Edda, did I hand you something? Must have left it in the car. You're looking so well I could bite you! Certainly trimmer. Is it bad form to say widowhood suits you?

HELÉNA:

Coffee, Edda.

EDDA:

Right away.

> *EDDA exits, closing the curtain to the kitchen after her.*

MUTZI:

Oooh, it's freezing in here — ! *(Stops and takes in the room. Can't hide she's rather horrified. Tries to cover, recognizing a piece of furniture)* I remember this! Used to be in your front hall, next to the — What's this? Are we laughing or crying? Now no tears. If you start, I'll have to join in, and I've just had my hair done.

HELÉNA:
Give me your hands. It's just seeing you again. Brings everything — You haven't changed. So beautiful. Now before I forget, I need to apologize for the state of the coffee, which is actually ersatz. And we've no whipped cream. In fact, I have very little hospitality to offer you —

MUTZI:
Oh shush! I'm here to see you. Besides, no one's taking whipped cream these days. *Mit schlag*[1] went out with gingerbread cookies. Now. I was trying to calculate this on the drive over: we last saw each other the summer at the lake, summer before last, which would make it eighteen months.

HELÉNA:
Yes. I lost the summer house after —

MUTZI:
Eighteen months! It isn't right! We must do something about that.

HELÉNA:
I thought that's what we're doing.

MUTZI:
Now listen. I know you're sick of hearing it — and I'm not saying it because I have to — after all, I did send you those flowers back when we all heard —

---

1. "With whipped cream"

No, I'm saying it because I love you and I want to express how sorry I am about Stefan. I don't like to think what I'd do if I ever lost Hermann (he's in Berlin on business but he sends his love. Some sort of nationalist uprising. It's a complete shambles). And before you say anything, I'm aware I should have called on you months ago when you were going through the worst of it, but you know how I am about death. I mean, aside from the sadness, aside from the grief which, let's face it, no one is going to feel to the same depth as you do, so why even try — aside from all that, death is just so — well, awkward.

HELÉNA:
They sent me his decoration.

MUTZI:
His — ?

HELÉNA:
The Knight's Cross of the Order of Franz Joseph.

The sound of the kettle whistling, off. The whistle fades.

MUTZI:
Oh, and the kitchen's through there: isn't that cozy. Heléna, I told you, I'm no good with death. I never know how to... And now you're looking at me oddly. Hermann said you'd be able to tell. I'm only four months gone but the doctors say it's going to be triplets.

HELÉNA:
What? Triplets? Mutzi, you mean, you're —

MUTZI:

No, I'm joking. Honestly! Sitting there all gloomy; I'm trying to make you smile. Triplets? And lose my figure and privacy for the next twenty years? I'd sooner walk to China. I've never had the maternal instinct. I know I should, but.... Then you and Stefan never had any. Children: that constant need they have. Like leeches. *(She shudders.)* Of course, Hermann dreams of being a father. Tries practically every night, which can't be normal.

HELÉNA:

You really are a troublemaker.

MUTZI:

(conspiratorial) Do you know what he says? In the middle of it. I swear to God. "It is one's patriotic duty to sire a son!"

HELÉNA:

He does not!

MUTZI:

And something about moral fortitude. Sometimes he cries.

> *The curtain opens and EDDA re-enters with a tray of coffee. She proceeds to serve.*

HELÉNA:

Ah! Here we are!

MUTZI:

I say to him, Hermann, do you expect me to personally repopulate Greater Austria? Edda, that smells divine.

HELÉNA:

That isn't the coffee we had in the — And whipped cream?

EDDA:

I wasn't about to let a special occasion go to waste. *Mit schlag,* Frau Fessendorf?

MUTZI:

Heavens no. Figures don't watch themselves. Wait. Did you — ? I'm sorry, yes, *mit schlag,* Edda, please.

HELÉNA:

Don't be silly. If you don't want *mit schlag,* you mustn't —

MUTZI:

I would! *Mit schlag!* And gingerbread cookies! Edda, you temptress.

> *The doorbell rings. EDDA hands out the coffee, then goes to answer the door and steps out.*

Where was I? Patriotism! What a notion. I understand allegiance to an Emperor, a king. There's a tradition. But what's this Republic ever done for me that I should give it sons? A woman without a title has no identity. Hermann hates it when I say that. But then, according to that Freud fellow, men only understand women as either mothers or whores.

HELÉNA:

(Spilling some of her coffee) Oh dear.

> *RUDY enters, carrying a small potted plant, with EDDA following.*

EDDA:

— I'm telling you, she has company. If you come back later —

RUDY:

I only want to give her her present.

EDDA:

(seeing the spill, going to Heléna's side) Here, let me do that.

MUTZI:

It seems you have a very eager young man awaiting you, Heléna.

EDDA:

I tried to stop him, but he would insist.

HELÉNA:

Countess von Fessendorf, may I present Rudy, our grocer's son.

MUTZI:

What has he got there? Crocuses? They're just beginning to open up and show their little faces. Just like you, Heléna. Isn't he handsome. Tell me — Rudy, is it? — do you bring flowers to all your customers?

RUDY:

I brought them for Frau Altman's birthday.

MUTZI:

Really! And do we know how old Frau Altman is today?

EDDA:

Rudy, put the flowers down and go.

MUTZI:

> *Vraiment? Tsk, quel dommage. Ce jeune homme, il est très beau, tu sait.*[1]

HELÉNA:

> *Arrête!*[2] Thank you, Rudy. They're lovely.
>
> > *During the following, RUDY offers an awkward bow and exits.*

HELÉNA:

> *Chérie, vous êtes terrible!*[3]

MUTZI:

> *Moi? Qu'est-ce que je fais?*[4]

HELÉNA:

> *Il est un enfant.*[5]

MUTZI:

> Where's your patriotism?
>
> > *The upstairs violinist launches into a painful rendition of Schrammel's "Wien bleibt Wien".*

HELÉNA:

> Oh good Lord. Edda, I thought I asked you to —

EDDA:

> *(exiting)* My apologies, Frau Altman. I'll take care of it immediately.

---

1. "Really? Tsk, how sad. That young man, he's very handsome, you know."
2. "Stop!"
3. "My dear, you're terrible!"
4. "Me? What did I do?"
5. "He's a child."

MUTZI:

What the devil is that? It isn't music, is it?

HELÉNA:

There's a child upstairs.

MUTZI:

Yes, and it sounds as though it's being murdered. Which reminds me: you must have heard. Lotte Grunwald? *(No reaction.) Ah Chérie, c'est un scandale!*[1] It's all anyone's talking about. Of course, some of us are trying to keep her name out of it. Out of respect for the memory of her dear father. I tell you, it's these filthy Reds. Relishing any opportunity to humiliate one of ours. Political revenge, plain and simple.

The music upstairs stops abruptly.

The police nabbed Lotte walking along the Gürtel with a Ukrainian or something at some godforsaken hour. "Nabbed" is the word they used. I can't believe you haven't heard. It even made the *Wiener Zeitung. (Nibbles a gingerbread cookie.)*

HELÉNA:

Yes, well, I don't take the newspapers as I used to.

MUTZI:

(Mouth full) She's utterly ruined. No one will help her, and what did she expect? Never did have much sense. The Captain of Police is calling it a social epidemic. Apparently, so many widows of fallen soldiers have taken to…walking the streets, they're rounding up any woman in full mourning

---

1. "Oh, my dear, it's a scandal!"

out alone after ten o'clock at night. You — haven't received her, have you?

HELÉNA:
I haven't seen Lotte for months.

MUTZI:
See you don't. Last thing you need is scandal just as you're reentering society. Oh, let's talk about something else. I was at *Zwieback & Bruder* the other day with some of the diplomatic wives and we found the darlingest little beaded clutch —

HELÉNA:
Things must have been very difficult for her.

MUTZI:
Things are difficult for everyone, Heléna, that doesn't mean she has to — If the poor fool had used her head, she'd have waited out her term of mourning and then relied on her friends to introduce her to some eligible and understanding gentleman instead of — degrading herself in such a —

HELÉNA:
I'm sure she only did it as a last resort; to try to save what life she had.

MUTZI:
Not exactly a life worth saving, if you ask me. Honestly, if her brother Jan had lived, he'd die in shame to see her now.

HELÉNA:
If Jan had lived, Lotte would have had no reason to walk the streets. She'd have had her family to

support her. But she has no one. Not a husband, not a brother: a whole generation, gone. All she has is that small child.

MUTZI:

I don't understand your tone. Are you defending her?

HELÉNA:

I have no tone. I'm defending no one. I simply... She used to be our good friend. Can we not show a little compassion? What if it were one of us?

MUTZI:

Oh now don't trot out "there but for the grace of God." It wouldn't be.

HELÉNA:

I said "what if."

MUTZI:

And I said "it wouldn't be."

HELÉNA:

Of course, you know best. You just be grateful you have Hermann.

MUTZI:

I am! Grateful I have Hermann. Four words I never thought I'd say. Ha! *(Stops.)* I don't know if you're aware of it, Heléna, but you've changed. Here I am, after eighteen months, coming to do you a good turn, and what do I find in place of my sweet girlhood chum but a very angry woman.

HELÉNA:

What do you mean, a good turn?

MUTZI:

A very angry woman.

> EDDA *re-enters, crosses, and exits into the kitchen, quietly closing the curtain after her.*

HELÉNA:

Mutzi, I am sorry. It's ridiculous of us to argue.

MUTZI:

I've always loved you, Heléna. You know that. And you're right: Lotte was once our friend. She was the funny one, I was the pretty one, and you were the one everyone respected. The smart one. I didn't mind being the pretty one, even though I knew smart and funny last forever and pretty is a gift of the moment. But I always felt you looked down at me because of that.

HELÉNA:

Looked down at you? Mutzi, I would never —

MUTZI:

You looked down at me. And then when Lotte and I fell out and it was just us, I felt it even more. But, as I said, I've always loved you. Which is why I'm here to do you a good turn in your time of need. When you're in no position to look down at me. So I want to hear you say you need my help. I want to look down at you for a change. Then I will tell you about the good turn I've come here to do.

> *Pause.*

HELÉNA:

Mutzi, I — I don't deserve your kindness. I need

your help.

MUTZI:

Heléna! Did you think I was being serious? Oh dear lord, you actually thought — ? I was trying to make you laugh! I forget how convincing I can be. All the same, I'm a little hurt that you'd believe I could be so cruel. The look on your face! It's really not fair of you at all. Especially considering the fact it's not all fiction! No, when I said I've come to do you a good turn, my little chum, I really meant that. And it's perfect, you see, because you'd be doing me a favor. Well, not so much a favor as — well — let me start at the beginning. It's like this —

SCENE THREE

Several nights later.

The room is dark and silent, save the ticking of the clock. A key in a lock.

HELÉNA bursts through the door, slamming it behind her, her hat and gloves in her hand, a rip in her dress. She is out of breath and shaking. She listens to make sure no one is on the other side of the door. Sensing she's safe, her breathing begins to slow. Touching her mouth, she discovers a bloody lip. She laughs. She starts to cry. She tries to regain her composure by singing to herself.

She produces a few wadded-up bills which she drops onto the table. She smooths them out and counts them.

SCENE FOUR

Late afternoon. A week later.

EDDA enters from the bedroom with Heléna's black dress which she has been mending. She is pouting, grunting, and slamming things. She opens the locked cabinet, pours herself a shot of schnapps. HELÉNA enters in gray. She watches as Edda knocks back the shot.

EDDA:
Can you honestly not see she's playing you for a fool?

HELÉNA:
She wants to introduce me to an eligible gentleman. Where is the harm?

EDDA:
(pouring another) I remember your dinner parties before the war: that woman would throw herself at every husband in the room, except her own. *(Knocks it back.)*

HELÉNA:
Two glasses qualifies as drinking on the job.

EDDA:

She's a nosy cow and a stinking gossip and I wouldn't trust her "good turn" as far as I could throw her — which, let me tell you, I am tempted to do!

HELÉNA:

(laughing) You used to frighten Stefan when you turned like this. Now give us a kiss and shut up; you're giving me a headache. Haven't you finished mending that tear?

EDDA:

(handing her a bonbon) I bought you a chocolate when I was out earlier.

HELÉNA:

Edda, you have got to stop spending your own money on me.

EDDA:

I didn't. That's your money.

> *HELÉNA unwraps and eats it. She is literally overcome with the pleasure of the taste of it.*

So who is it Miss Nosy-Pants has in mind for you?

HELÉNA:

He's some friend or colleague of Hermann's. I forget.

EDDA:

Another ham hock.

HELÉNA:

Shall I tell you my suspicion? I believe Mutzi is in love with him — this man — and I am merely to provide the veneer of propriety so that she can flirt with him *sans souci.*[1]

EDDA:
But this is exactly what I mean. It's a trap!

HELÉNA:
(laughing) A trap? You ought to go on the stage.

EDDA:
Listen to me, I know women, and one way or another that harpy is going to see to it you end up to blame for something you didn't do.

HELÉNA:
Edda, I don't care! Tonight I'm going to the Philharmonic. When was the last time I went to the Philharmonic? Or the opera? Or the theatre? The nearest thing I've had to poetry or music for the past eighteen months has been that child of Satan! I need to meet new people. I need to hear voices and laughter or I don't know how I'm going to —

> *EDDA opens her mouth to speak but changes her mind. Still angry, she folds her arms.*

If it's meant to be, then it shall be. If not, then what's the harm? I'll meet him at the concert, we'll hear some good music... And you're to say nothing about my suspicion, understand?

EDDA:
Who do I talk to.

HELÉNA:
<u>Look how </u>Rudy's crocuses are coming in.

1. "without worry."

EDDA:

I don't want to see you hurt, that's all.

HELÉNA:

You mend that dress and I'll be fine.

EDDA:

(nagging the dress) Did you know, in medieval days, instead of black, they wore white for mourning? The French called it *deuil blanc.* Also in Japan, apparently. Professor Pinchik was telling me about it. I wouldn't care for that. How could you grieve properly, all the time worried about spilling something?

HELÉNA:

So we're striking up conversations with gentlemen, are we?

EDDA:

What do you mean? Professor Pinchik? I ran into him at Zuckermaier's. He's a very intelligent man.

HELÉNA:

I think it's awfully sweet!

EDDA:

I'm going to stick you with this needle.

HELÉNA:

And I'm wagering there's another chocolate in your apron. If you give it to me, I'll say no more about your boyfriend.

EDDA:

He's not my — !

> *EDDA tsks and sighs and gives her another chocolate.*

HELÉNA pockets it.

(Mending) Anyway, you should throw this damn thing out. You said you wouldn't wear black again once you transitioned to half-mourning.

HELÉNA:
I may still need it. I may not like the world I see out there.

EDDA:
Enough of that. You'll take to it like a duck to water. You'll see.

HELÉNA:
Do you remember when Captain Altman and I were first married?

EDDA:
How you two loved to go dancing. Coming home at all hours. All that laughter. It was a different world.

HELÉNA:
You saw us. Were we in love?

EDDA:
You were both young and incredibly stupid. It's easier for stupid people to be in love. I don't know why, but it is.

HELÉNA:
He cut such a handsome figure. My golden Stefan. He was... He'd walk into a room and all eyes would be on him. He was everything I learned to wish for. I loved him for being that.

EDDA:

By the way — (*She draws from a pocket a handful of cash and holds it out, not looking at it.*) You left this money lying about. Best put it away before it gets lost.

HELÉNA:

Oh! Right! I — (*A beat.*) I shouldn't be going out. I shouldn't have said yes. I don't want to leave the house. All I want to do is sleep. I wish I could sleep for a hundred years! And then, when I wake up, everything will be solved and sorted.

EDDA:

(*holding out the dress*) There you are. Good as new. You never did tell me how you tore it.

HELÉNA:

Hang it in the wardrobe.

> *EDDA exits into the bedroom with the dress. HELÉNA is lost in thought when a timid knock at the door startles her. HELÉNA panics.*

Edda — ? Who is it?

RUDY:

(*off*) Rudy.

HELÉNA:

Who?

RUDY:

(*off*) Rudy from Zuckermaier's, Frau Altman.

HELÉNA:

Rudy!

> *HELÉNA opens the door. RUDY stands in the doorway with a basket of food, nicely packed.*

RUDY:

The food you ordered. And I found a nice old basket for it all.

HELÉNA:

Oh good! Yes, come in. Shhh! I don't want Edda knowing about this.

> *RUDY enters, staring at her, enchanted. HELÉNA shuts the door after him and goes to the table and finds paper to write on.*

RUDY:

You're looking very lovely, Frau Altman.

HELÉNA:

Hm? Oh, I'm going to the Philharmonic. Can you believe it? Now, you remember everything I told you?

RUDY:

Of course.

HELÉNA:

You take this down to the station and tell them it's for the person whose name I'm writing on this paper. If anyone asks who sent it, you plead ignorance.

RUDY:

But they're the police, Frau Altman. I can't lie to the police.

HELÉNA:

A secret isn't a lie, Rudy. Now what have we got?

RUDY:

Some Semmel rolls with cold cuts. Würstel and

mustard. A pot of Liptauer cheese. A jar of beef consommé.

HELÉNA:

(producing the bonbon and putting it in the basket) And here's a little chocolate for the child. *(Handing him money and the note)* Now this should cover it, plus a bit extra for you. And here's the name.

RUDY:

(reading the note) Lotte Grunwald. Is she a friend of yours? Is she in trouble?

HELÉNA:

Remember, this is our secret.

RUDY:

You should write her a note. Every secret mission's got to have a note. Besides, if I were your friend, I'd be happy indeed to know this came from you.

HELÉNA:

But the police —

RUDY:

I'll get it past them. Trust me.

HELÉNA:

What should I write?

The doorbell rings.

Oh good God. No, no, don't open it!

EDDA:

(re-entering) Rudy! I didn't hear you come in. What's that you got there?

HELÉNA:

He was just on his way out.

EDDA:

(re: the basket) Is that for us? I didn't send for anything.

RUDY:

(flustered) No, it's — I mixed up the orders. It's a mistake.

EDDA:

That's not like you to make a mistake. Let me see, is that the name?

> *The doorbell rings again. HELÉNA has quickly finished scribbling out a note and intervenes.*

HELÉNA:

Edda, leave him be! Answer the door.

> *EDDA stares at Heléna, affronted. HELÉNA exits into the bedroom, but not before getting the note to RUDY in a clandestine way. Doorbell rings and holds. EDDA answers. MUTZI.*

MUTZI:

Did I wake you?

EDDA:

Frau Fessendorf.

MUTZI:

I've been out here so long, I'm putting down roots. Is Heléna ready? *(Entering, seeing Rudy)* I know you: Reuben, isn't it? What, another gift for Frau Altman?

EDDA:

He got his deliveries mixed up. Now let me see that name.

RUDY:

I'm sorry. I can't.

EDDA:

I beg your pardon?

RUDY:

I can't...reveal personal information about other customers. At Zuckermaier's one may depend on... discretion. *(Going)* I'm sorry.

MUTZI:

Just one moment there! This is all rather intriguing. A mystery basket, eh, Edda? I love solving a good mystery. Now Reuben, you hand me that paper like a good boy. Come, you can trust me; my husband's a diplomat.

RUDY:

Of course, Frau Fessendorf. Is that a new hat? *(With effort)* C'est très charmant.[1]

MUTZI:

You're changing the subject, young man.

RUDY:

Not at all. Only... Well, pardon me for saying so, but your eyes, Frau Fessendorf —

MUTZI:

My eyes?

---

1. "It's very charming."

RUDY:
Yes.

MUTZI:
What's wrong with my eyes?

RUDY:
They're brighter this evening. Is that possible?

MUTZI:
Is it? Are they?

RUDY:
I can only think it's because of that certain shade of your new hat. *(Producing from the basket)* Please accept this bonbon as a token of my admiration. *(As she accepts the chocolate, he kisses her hand.)* Your servant, Madam.

RUDY exits. MUTZI watches him go.

MUTZI:
Now that boy has an eye. I've always been good with hats.

EDDA:
Unbelievable.

MUTZI:
How old did you say he was? What!

HELÉNA:
(entering) Are you being wicked out here?

MUTZI:
Ah! Here we are — *(kissing her)* and we're in gray! — *(other cheek)*.

HELÉNA:

Just give me one moment to get on my hat and we'll be off.

EDDA:

Will your husband be joining you, Frau Fessendorf?

HELÉNA:

Yes, where is Hermann? I've been looking forward to seeing him.

MUTZI:

He's in Rotterdam. Some last-minute diplomatic business. It's just as well. The Philharmonic puts him to sleep and then I have to be on the alert or he snores like a blast-furnace.

HELÉNA:

You mean it's to be just the three of us?

MUTZI:

It'll be fine — though I believe we're in for an all-Mahler program. Messy Judaic emotionalism. And don't get your hopes up. About Béla. He's a very complicated man. Oh, he told me the funniest joke — how did it go?

EDDA:

(exiting) Was it about a third wheel?

HELÉNA:

I won't be a moment.

> HELÉNA exits after EDDA into the bedroom. MUTZI looks around the room in general distaste, humming Strauss's "Wiener Blut," ending up at the

mirror. The Man — the same as in Scene One — appears in the open doorway. His name is BÉLA. He is silent and wary of entering.

BÉLA:
Your friend... She lives here?

MUTZI:
Someone took his sweet time! Did you have trouble parking the Mercedes? She's putting on her hat. Yes, I know! The place looks like something out of the final act of a Puccini opera. But you mustn't hover in the doorway, Béla, it's unmannerly. *(Kisses him on the cheek.)* What's the matter? You're white as a sheet. Don't tell me you took the stairs? You men are absurd! It's a dreadful building, but there's a perfectly good lift.

BÉLA:
I should go. I shouldn't be here.

MUTZI:
The concert doesn't start 'til seven. We've plenty of time.

BÉLA:
You don't understand. She won't want to meet me.

MUTZI:
Ah, *taisez-vous!*[1] The poor thing's been pining since I suggested it. Now remember, you must be very careful with her. She's the fragile sort. Wasn't raised to survive on her own. Like a wounded bird lost in a wood.

---

1. "Be quiet!"

BÉLA:

I can't help that and I'm sorry. You simply have to take my word on it. Extend to her my apologies —

MUTZI:

Absolutely not! You know perfectly well Heléna and I can't go to the Philharmonic unaccompanied. It isn't done.

BÉLA:

You don't understand.

MUTZI:

(slipping folded money into his coat breast pocket) Here's a few thousand Kronen. You can buy us a coffee at the interval. Now give me a smile and save your moping for Mahler. You'll have his whole Second Symphony to brood through. What's the name of it? "Reservations"?

> *HELÉNA has entered with a hat. And EDDA. BÉLA turns his back, pretending to study the coal stove.*

HELÉNA:

I believe it's called, "The Resurrection."

MUTZI:

Is it? All I know is, it's long and it's loud!

HELÉNA:

(checking hat in mirror) It's the first time I'll have been out in society for over a year and a half: if that isn't a resurrection — ! *(Seeing Béla)* Oh! — Hello.

MUTZI:

Heléna Altman, allow me to introduce Béla Hoyos. But you Hungarians say it surname-first, don't you?

Hoyos Béla.

BÉLA:

(*shaking her hand*) I adore Mahler. One of the few artists who understood the dialectical complexity of the modern European character. Viennese audiences never fully appreciated him while he was alive. Once at the Cafe Landtmann, I sat at a table next to him and his wife. I kept straining to eavesdrop, to pick up any casually dropped pearl of wisdom. All I managed was, "The clientele here has really dropped off."

> MUTZI, *who has heard it before, joined in on the final few words and laughs.* HELÉNA *laughs.*

HELÉNA:

I'm sorry, I thought we were to meet you at the concert.

MUTZI:

That was the original plan. But the thought of saddling myself all night with my wretched driver (I think he takes cocaine. I'm kidding!), well — seemed so much nicer to have Béla behind the wheel. And, of course, he knows all the best shortcuts.

HELÉNA:

Hoyos? Forgive me, only you seem somehow familiar. Did you know my husband?

MUTZI:

Perhaps you recognize his name. Béla writes for the *Arbeiter-Zeitung*. Though you mustn't hold that against him. He may be a Socialist, but he assures me he's one of the good ones.

BÉLA:

I'm sure Frau Altman doesn't take the workers' newspapers.

HELÉNA:

(with a laugh) I'm afraid I don't. As a matter of fact, I haven't —

> *And it suddenly comes to HELÉNA and she remembers and she starts back as though stung.*

BÉLA:

Shall we be on our way?

MUTZI:

I've told you, Béla: we've plenty of time.

EDDA:

(rushing to her side, concerned) Frau Altman?

MUTZI:

I have no intention of arriving early. It shows desperation.

BÉLA:

Perhaps I — I should run on ahead and get the car started. I'll be —

> *BÉLA exits.*

EDDA:

Frau Altman, are you all right? What's happened?

MUTZI:

What's going on? Béla, wait, I'm with you! Heléna, come! *(Exiting)* Béla?

> *EDDA has helped HELÉNA to a chair. She rushes to the locked cabinet. Pours a shot of schnapps and brings it to her. HELÉNA stares blankly.*

EDDA:
Drink. *(No response.)* Drink!

> *HELÉNA relents and drinks.*

It takes time to rejoin the world, Frau Altman. You mustn't overwhelm yourself. You'll be fine once you're seated and the music starts. He's a handsome man. They're waiting. You'd best be on your way.

> *HELÉNA slowly rises. She exits.*

ACT TWO

In an older overgrown section of the Zentralfriedhof, the largest cemetery in Vienna.

Under a tree, near a mausoleum, runs a path. Just beyond this path and through a weed-choked tumbledown metal gate, among old headstones, there is a small clearing. On it stands a new well-tended but very simple stone bench opposite a memorial marker bearing the name "Altman."

SCENE ONE

Early morning, five days later.

HELÉNA, in gray half-mourning, is on the ground before the memorial, her face in her hands, her hat and gloves on the bench. Outside the gate, reading tombstones, is BÉLA. Silence.

BÉLA:
(reading from tombstones) "Wife"… That's the only word on this headstone. No name, no dates. *(A beat.)* That one must be the husband. The one that says, "Miser."

HELÉNA:
Please — go away!

BÉLA:
You shouldn't be sitting on the cold ground. Influenza's very popular these days. *(A beat. Another tombstone)* "Sophie von Faninal. Aged 26. Soon shall your slumbering dust arise, to join the triumph of the skies."

HELÉNA:
What do you want from me?

BÉLA:

To talk.

HELÉNA:

What could you and I possibly have to talk about?

BÉLA:

What did you think of the Mahler? The other night.

HELÉNA:

I hated it. I could have the police on you. Menacing. That's what you're doing.

BÉLA:

That isn't true.

HELÉNA:

You've been following me for five nights...!

BÉLA:

The Mahler. I don't believe you hated it.

HELÉNA:

It was vulgar and intrusive. Like you.

BÉLA steps up to her with a flask.

BÉLA:

May I offer you —

HELÉNA, startled, cries out.

HELÉNA:

Get away from me! Get out! This is my husband's plot. You have no right to —

BÉLA:

I'm so sorry. I didn't mean to —

HELÉNA:
Get on the other side of that fence.

BÉLA steps back through the fence.

BÉLA:
I only meant to offer you some brandy. It's a chilly morning.

HELÉNA:
(A beat) Herr Hoyos, have you told Mutzi von Fessendorf how we met?

BÉLA:
No.

HELÉNA:
Are you going to?

BÉLA:
Why would I do that?

HELÉNA:
It would ruin me.

BÉLA:
As I said, why would I do that?

HELÉNA:
You'd rather hold it over my head. Threaten to put my name in the papers and make me a public disgrace as you did to my friend Lotte.

BÉLA:
Who? I'm not that sort of journalist, Frau Altman —

HELÉNA:
Do you know what that would do? Do you know

how hard I've —

BÉLA:

— I write trifles, commentary, odd matters of interest; what the French call Feuilleton.

HELÉNA:

I have no money if it's blackmail you're thinking. Or was it to be payment in another form?

BÉLA:

That's very dramatic. Though I suppose it's to be expected.

HELÉNA:

Herr Hoyos, don't be grand. That night of the concert, after you drove us home, I know you came back to my apartments. I know it was you knocking at one in the morning. For the past five nights, you've followed me. Every time I stopped, you hovered, scaring away any... *(She trails off.)*

BÉLA:

Have some brandy. You're shivering. Go on; you can keep being angry with me, but it'll warm you up.

HELÉNA:

I'm not angry. I simply want you to leave me be.

BÉLA:

And that's the part I don't understand. We've been officially introduced. Everything is right and correct. No one needs to know how we first met.

HELÉNA:

You expect me to take your word on that.

BÉLA:

Try me. *(Holding out the flask)* Tessék.[1] I'm really not a bad person.

HELÉNA:

You go to prostitutes.

BÉLA:

Now who's being grand? And your use of the plural makes rather an assumption.

HELÉNA:

You want me to believe our meeting was your first?

BÉLA:

So it was a correct assumption.

HELÉNA:

How many? If you're an honest man, you'll tell the truth.

BÉLA:

Isn't that rather personal? *(A beat.)* Three. You — I mean, we — that was the third.

HELÉNA:

(Considers. Reaches out a hand) I'll have some of that brandy.

BÉLA:

I'll have to step onto holy soil.

> *Almost having gotten her to smile, BÉLA re-enters through the gate and hands her the flask. She studies him before deciding to drink.*

May I ask where he fell? Your husband.

---

1. "Have some."

HELÉNA:
Did you serve?

BÉLA:
I saw my share of battle.

HELÉNA:
(Pause.) Captain Altman died near Ypres. He was awarded a posthumous decoration. His body was lost to a grenade.

She takes a sip of the brandy.

BÉLA:
September of '18, wasn't it? Only two months before the Armistice. *(Off her look)* I have a colleague in the Casualties Department of the War Archive. I had him look it up.

HELÉNA:
You had someone look me up? My husband?

BÉLA:
I was curious. You had my interest piqued. His decoration. The Order of Franz Joseph, wasn't it? Knight's Cross. Used to be quite prestigious. Till the end of the war, that is, when they gave them away like kittens. What is heroism, anyway? Are you required to be dead? You may as well give a pig a medal the next time you dine on a schnitzel. On the other hand, if he'd survived, if he'd lived to come home and care for you so that you wouldn't be... doing what you have to do —

HELÉNA:
Being menaced by the likes of you.

BÉLA:

Exactly! Then would he be a hero worthy of a medal. It's the living who should be honored. The dead gain nothing by it. Do I shock you?

HELÉNA:

Tell me, Herr Hoyos, how do you come to know the von Fessendorfs?

BÉLA:

Hermann I know because my newspaper enjoys covering his bumbling reactionary diplomacy. What an embarrassing relic he is.

HELÉNA:

And Mutzi?

BÉLA:

Mutzi I first met at a reception for some ambassador or other. I'll admit, I was charmed. She has the irresistible charisma of true lunacy. The more we spoke, the more I felt these invisible hawk-like talons closing around me. Before I knew it, I "simply had to" join her for supper, and then I "simply had to" accompany her to the theatre, and then... Then I started seeing that look in her eyes. That hot and eager look that says she's falling in love. And there's nothing you can do to stop it.

HELÉNA:

Of course you can stop it. It's the height of cruelty not to.

BÉLA:

To your knowledge, has Mutzi ever been denied anything?

HELÉNA:

So what do you propose to do about it?

BÉLA:

You're implying it's my responsibility?

HELÉNA:

I'm asking what you plan to do. You say you're not a bad person; what sort of man are you?

BÉLA:

The sort who would like to know you better.

HELÉNA:

How can I make this clear, Herr Hoyos? That sentiment is not reciprocated.

BÉLA:

Come now, surely you must have some curiosity. Or has grief erased all interest in your fellow human beings? You can't be that resigned from life. One question. Anything.

Pause.

HELÉNA:

What was it you liked about the Mahler?

BÉLA:

Wasn't it wonderful? He's the only true successor to Beethoven. Single-handedly destroys the symphonic form by taking it to its endpoint. After Mahler, there can never be another symphony.

HELÉNA:

Ours is an age of definitives. They say the same about the war: the war to end all wars. There really would be dancing in the streets if that were true.

BÉLA:

Not in Vienna. Here, they don't approve of tinkering with tradition. Here, war and music will always be in fashion and always in three-four time. How's the brandy?

HELÉNA:

(handing him back the flask) Very good. Thank you.

BÉLA:

Have some more.

HELÉNA:

And end up drunk at this hour of the morning?

BÉLA:

Ah, but to us, Frau Altman, it is still night. We've been walking for hours. If you look carefully, you can still discern where the stars have stood.

HELÉNA:

There's a phrase. Let me guess: in your spare time you write sentimental poetry. I knew it. Doesn't that rather go against your grain as a socialist?

BÉLA:

Socialism is deeply sentimental, Frau Altman. When we care for the hungry old woman next door, when we build homes for our veterans and our destitute, when we fight for fairness and equality in our courts, we're being good socialists. And what could be more sentimental?

HELÉNA:

(pause) You talk too much.

BÉLA:

It's true. It's probably one of these new — what are they called? Neurotic impulses. I try to control it, but I can't stop.

HELÉNA:

(laughing) What am I going to do with you, Herr Hoyos?

BÉLA:

Make love to me. I want to feel you again.

HELÉNA:

I think you'd better leave.

BÉLA:

You make me dizzy. Heléna —

HELÉNA:

Go home and lie down.

BÉLA:

I'd rather lie down with you. Here in the dirt.

HELÉNA:

This is my husband's memorial!

BÉLA:

So? He isn't buried here. I kept your smell on me for two days. I'd close my eyes and think of you and pleasure myself.

HELÉNA:

Have you no decency?

BÉLA:

Of course not, I'm Hungarian. *(Producing money)* Look, I can pay. For your time, I mean. If that's a consideration.

HELÉNA:
Did I ask you for money? Did I make any suggestion that —

BÉLA:
Take it! I don't want anything for it. I wouldn't touch you without your consent.

HELÉNA:
You won't be touching me at all.

BÉLA:
You hate the thought of it, don't you? The memory of me inside you.

HELÉNA:
Stop it.

BÉLA:
I knew it even that night. The greater your disgust, the more I wanted you. I wanted to prove myself. That I could give you pleasure.

HELÉNA:
I won't listen to this!

BÉLA:
Insane, I know. But there we are. Next thing I know, I'm out on the street and I can't get you out of my mind. For five and a half weeks, I knew where you lived, but did I set foot in your direction? It had been a business transaction and the privacy of business must always be respected. Then, out of the blue, I'm driving Mutzi to pick up her widowed little friend for the Philharmonic and she's directing me to your apartments.

A distant roll of thunder, drawing nearer.

HELÉNA:
That does not bode well.

BÉLA:
Sounds like rain.

HELÉNA:
Please don't. I'll be soaked to the bone by the time I get home.

BÉLA:
Here — *(Removing his jacket, he places it over her shoulders.)* There's a ledge. We can stand under that.

> *Another roll of thunder, nearer, and they run under the overhang of the mausoleum.*

My money says it's a freak spring rain. We have a saying in Hungary: if the sun is shining bright while it's raining, the Devil is beating his wife.

HELÉNA:
You're a barbaric people — *(Staring out, reaching out)* — but apparently very good weathermen.

BÉLA:
And there's that scent of yours once more. Intoxicating.

HELÉNA:
That isn't me; that's the rain.

> *BÉLA tries to kiss HELÉNA.*

What are you —

> *BÉLA loses his footing. He falls against the metal door*

> *of the mausoleum, which gives way. He falls into the mausoleum.*

(Laughing) You clumsy — ! Are you all right? Béla? Béla?

> *HELÉNA steps into the mausoleum. Another roll of thunder, this one moving far away. From off stage, the sound of a car approaching. It stops. A door opens and shuts. Silence. Then —*

MUTZI:

(Off; calling) Yoo-hoo!...Heléna — ? *(After a moment, she wanders on outside the gate, carrying a light umbrella)* Are you there? Yoo-hoo...! Heléna, if you're there, don't make me walk through these gates! You know I can't abide cemeteries.

> *HELÉNA emerges from the mausoleum. MUTZI sees her and starts.*

Oh! You scared the daylights out of me. I thought you were a ghost.

HELÉNA:

I stepped in to avoid the rain. What are you doing here, Mutzi?

MUTZI:

In there? Heléna, there's dust on your — *(crossing herself)* Dear Christ, that could be someone's remains!

HELÉNA:

(brushing herself off) Mutzi, how did you find me? What do you want?

MUTZI:

I called at your apartments. Edda said, sometimes you come here to think. I can't imagine how.

HELÉNA:

And?

MUTZI:

And what?

HELÉNA:

What is it that's so urgent that you had to find me?

MUTZI:

Urgent? It isn't — It's — My, but aren't you stern. You've been very cold to me since the Philharmonic last Friday. You and Béla both. *(Breaking)* Heléna, I haven't heard from him and I don't understand! I sent around several notes. Even tried him on the telephone. His landlady says he's been out every night this week. He's usually so attentive. Where could he be? I tell you, it's torture: this silence, this —

> *MUTZI trails off in shock as BÉLA steps out of the mausoleum.*

This is embarrassing. I don't know what to say.

BÉLA:

Shall we try a good morning?

MUTZI:

How much of that did you hear? All of it. I'm mortified. *(A beat. Looking from Béla to Heléna and back again)* But why are you — ?

BÉLA:

Funny you should ask. *(A beat.)* I was out playing cards 'til about an hour ago. Lost nine games in a row. A defeat of symphonic proportions which put me in mind of Beethoven. I decided to pay my respects at his grave. Four sections over that way. Frau Altman was here dutifully tending her husband's memorial. I stopped to say hello, it threatened to rain, we took shelter.

MUTZI:

In a crypt. Together.

BÉLA:

There are no cafés about. Where would you recommend?

MUTZI:

May I have a word with you alone, Béla?

BÉLA:

Alone? Is that necessary?

MUTZI:

If you don't mind. I believe I'm entitled to an explanation. Unless I'm interrupting something here.

HELÉNA:

I should be going.

BÉLA:

No, please —

MUTZI:

What exactly —

BÉLA:

Is that a skull by your feet?

> *MUTZI cries out and jumps away, only to see there is nothing there. BÉLA chuckles.*

MUTZI:

That isn't funny! Why would you laugh? Why would you scare me like that? *(Pause.)* I took you for a gentleman. I know we have our social differences but even so, it never crossed my mind you'd have a cruel nature. Is that who you are? And you — Oh, I recognize that look. There's a lesson for me: no good deed goes unpunished. I can't wait till Hermann gets home from Rotterdam.

BÉLA:

Frau Fessendorf, if I have disappointed you in any way, or led you to believe in what is not, berate me, cut me off. In fact, if I have shown you any cruelty, then I insist you never deign to speak to me again. But let me be clear: this has nothing to do with Frau Altman, a woman of integrity and honor, who struggles daily under the heavy yoke of widowhood.

> *HELÉNA burst out in laughter but quickly disguises it as tears*

See how raw her pain? Now if you'll excuse me, I must needs sleep off my gambling losses. I trust we've seen the last of that pesky raincloud. *Kezét csókolom*[1], dear ladies. *Kezét csókolom.*

> *BÉLA gives a slight bow and exits, singing the tune of a Strauss waltz. Perhaps "Weiner blut." The women watch*

---

1. "I kiss your hand"; i.e. a polite hello or goodbye.

him go. MUTZI *looks at* HELÉNA. HELÉNA *looks away.*

SCENE TWO

A few nights later. Late.

BÉLA and HELÉNA enter, walking quickly along the path. When they reach the mausoleum, they hide along the side of it.

BÉLA:

(*entering; whispering*) Quickly — ! Quickly — !

HELÉNA:

(*whispering*) ...Is he still there? No, don't look!

BÉLA:

(*whispering*) Stop hitting me! I can see him. He's crouching low to the ground.

HELÉNA:

(*whispering*) Why is he crouching low to the ground?

BÉLA:

He's... Never mind, it's a bush.

HELÉNA:

What? Béla, I have not been eluding a bush. That copper saw my face!

> *BÉLA laughs.*

This is no laughing matter!

BÉLA:
Copper?

HELÉNA:
Policeman. Wait — is that him?

BÉLA:
I love that you're up on the lingo. And this cloak-and-dagger business of hiding in doorways: it's very erotic. Ow! Stop it!

HELÉNA:
You've got to stop following me; you'll get us both arrested.

BÉLA:
Why would anyone arrest us? We're a perfectly respectable couple, out for a night stroll. Arthur Schnitzler and his wife do it all the time.

HELÉNA:
(producing from her pocket a small handful of money) Take this back. Don't look at me with that ridiculous expression. I know you put this money in my coat pocket when you thought I wasn't looking.

BÉLA:
I don't know what you're talking about. *(A beat.)* Oh put that away. I want you to have it. If you don't take it, it'll simply end up going to card games or whores. Wait. That wasn't supposed to come out like that.

HELÉNA:

I knew you were lying. You said there'd been three.

BÉLA:

I'd never lie to you.

HELÉNA:

Three.

BÉLA:

This year.

HELÉNA:

Béla, it's March. That's one a month.

BÉLA:

What can I say? I've never been good with money. Soon as I get any, I get rid of it.

HELÉNA:

So you go to prostitutes because you don't understand economics? Let me explain it to you, my socialist friend: money is power.

BÉLA:

My God, you're beautiful. Why push me away? I want to know everything about you, Heléna. Your dreams. Your fears. What was it like? The first time you did it for money.

HELÉNA:

Go home. We both know what this is. You're chasing a fantasy, and the range of your affection begins and ends with pity. I'm but a means to reinforce your self-image as a Good Socialist; as Someone Who Cares.

BÉLA:

Is that really what you think of me?

HELÉNA:

(a pause; considering, then) Between the stack of worthless war bonds and the pittance of a state subsidy due my husband's military rank, I could barely... I had to sell everything we owned to pay the rent, the grocery bill, the coal bill... for this memorial! I couldn't sleep for worrying. So I'd go out walking. One night, I found myself by the canal. The water looked so... peaceful. I thought of throwing myself in. Then, somehow, suddenly there was this man. He kept talking to me. "I can be of assistance." I couldn't understand at first. He was from Budapest, like you. He reeked of cigarettes and sauerkraut. He called me "Ági."[1] Afterwards I wanted to vomit up my heart.

BÉLA:

When you were a little girl, what did you want to do with your life?

HELÉNA:

(with an ironic laugh) When I was a girl, I wanted to grow up to marry D'Artagnan. From "The Three Musketeers." Go on, laugh. *(He doesn't.)* My friend Lotte and I, that was our plan. We'd all live together in a big castle and have dozens of children and summer would never end.

BÉLA:

And was Captain Stefan Altman your D'Artagnan? I picture him more as an Athos or an Aramis.

---

1. Short for Ágnes.

HELÉNA:

But then we never did have any children.

BÉLA:

(tapping out cocaine) Children seem more interesting than they actually are. Once you talk to one, you realize they're really quite dull and stupid. *(Snorts coke.)*

HELÉNA:

What is that? Is that snuff?

BÉLA:

Tessék.[1] Try some.

HELÉNA:

(Snorts. Reacts) Oh! *(Laughing)* It's trickling down the back of my — Now the roof of my mouth is numb! What is this? Did you just give me cocaine?

BÉLA:

And on the sacred ground of your husband's memorial, no less.

HELÉNA:

You're unbelievable.

BÉLA:

If you don't embrace life, Heléna, it goes on without you.

HELÉNA:

Let it go on! Let it parade its way out of town. I'll stay here like Patience on a monument until — *(Stubs her toe against a grave. The sound of pain.)* My toe!

---

1. "Here you are."

BÉLA:
Did it fall off?

HELÉNA:
I stubbed it.

BÉLA:
Come, take your shoes off. Run your feet through the grass. It'll feel better in no time. Here, allow me.

HELÉNA:
No, you may not touch my feet! There are parts of the body that are — stop it: feet are different. Besides, mine are hideous.

BÉLA:
I don't believe you.

HELÉNA:
(after a beat) Fine. *(She watches him as he removes her shoes.)* I've never met anyone quite like you, Herr Hoyos.

BÉLA:
That's rather the point, isn't it?

HELÉNA:
My turn: The night we first met, what had you been doing? Before.

BÉLA:
I'd gone out to dinner with a friend. *(He stares at her feet.)*

HELÉNA:
I feel naked. No, go on: look at them. I don't care what you think.

BÉLA:

These feet of yours, Heléna, are without a doubt, two of the ugliest things I have ever laid eyes on in my life. Don't cover your face. You're so pretty on that end.

HELÉNA:

What are you doing?

BÉLA:

Rubbing them. Just because they're ugly doesn't mean they shouldn't feel good. Your toes. The arch of your foot.

HELÉNA:

This "friend" you went to dinner with. A woman?

BÉLA:

A fellow journalist. We went to the Cafe Herrenhof. Have you been? It's quite the scene. Warring factions encamped mere tables from each other. A battlefield of wits, where no-man's-land is dotted with Linzertortes. A skirmish broke out over Austro-Germanic unification. Champagne was spilled. It was a sight of bloodied reputations. I saw home my friend as he'd suffered a severe blow to his pride.

HELÉNA:

(laughing) Did you memorize this?

BÉLA:

It behooves a journalist to have a photographic eye.

HELÉNA:

My God, you're annoying.

BÉLA:

But you enjoy it? Say you do. You have a magnificent ankle.

HELÉNA:

Finish your story.

BÉLA:

That's when I saw you: a vision walking through the mists of night, eyes clapped to the pavement, sorrowful as Niobe.

HELÉNA:

I'm going to regret this, but — Niobe?

BÉLA:

Greek mythology. Her husband and fourteen children were murdered by Artemis and Apollo. She cried so much, she turned into a rock.

HELÉNA:

Artemis and Apollo, they're gods and goddesses, yet they behave like petty, vindictive children. If we must have them, shouldn't gods represent the better qualities?

BÉLA:

You mean like Jesus? He showed kindness to whores.

HELÉNA:

Does it give you pleasure, using that word?

BÉLA:

It's horrible, isn't it? "Kindness." You have very sensual calves.

HELÉNA:

Béla, what are you doing?

BÉLA:

Bringing you back from the dead. Your thigh —

HELÉNA:

That's enough.

BÉLA:

Shhh! Let me show you kindness, Heléna.

HELÉNA:

Béla, please —

BÉLA:

Let me. Let me.

> *He reaches further. She gasps. Leans in to him. Their faces are inches apart, their lips parted, as he pleasures her with his hand. It is an intense, vulnerable journey.*

HELÉNA:

Kiss me.

SCENE THREE

A week later. Afternoon.

EDDA and RUDY can be heard approaching. They enter, each carrying the handle of a large wicker basket which RUDY will proceed to unpack, setting out a blanket and all the requirements for a picnic, including plates, food, bottles of wine, glasses. EDDA will help a bit, but mostly she will supervise. RUDY has a black eye.

RUDY:
It's the sort of gate you need both hands to unlatch. So I put down my delivery box to open it, and these four fellows come round the corner, pretending to be friendly in that mocking way you know means trouble. Two of them I knew. Here? My father'd caught them stealing. One of the others had a broken-off billiard cue. "You're the son of that Jew Zuckermaier," he says. Someone else says, "He's got no mother. He's a Jew bastard." I'm about to correct them; to say, I did so have a mother. But it somehow feels insulting to her memory if I mention her in front of them, so I say nothing. They start in saying, "All Jews are bastards." They

get very philosophical. Should I put out the wine? The one with the broken cue pokes me in the ribs. "You're the reason we lost the war," he says. "You're the reason they took away our empire." Again, I want to correct him; to tell him how dearly my father loved the Kaiser; that the first great tragedy of his life was Sisi's assassination and the second, the death of my mother; that when we lost the empire, he lost his will to live. But they see I'm not going to say anything, so they start pulling the groceries out of the box and throwing them into the street. It's when I try to stop them that they hit me.

EDDA:

Professor Pinchik says when you got back to the shop you wouldn't tell anybody what happened. Rudy, it's not your fault those idiots ganged up on you.

RUDY:

He's keen on you, isn't he? The Professor.

EDDA:

Don't change the subject, and mind what you're doing. Frau Altman doesn't need her dishes cracked. Even if she is cracked in the head. Look at this place! Of all the spots in our beautiful city to sit and eat. It's bad luck, I told her. Eat in a cemetery, you'll give birth to a dead child.

RUDY:

I keep thinking about that boy with the broken cue. I wish he had stabbed me. I wish the four of them had killed me right there on the street, and my blood had run into the gutters. Then you'd know. Then you'd all be sorry.

EDDA:
What the devil? I'm not listening to another word of this nonsense.

> *RUDY grabs for one of EDDA's breasts. She looks at his hand. She looks at him.*

What are you looking for?

RUDY:
(breaking away and crying) No one's ever going to love me.

EDDA:
Not if you go around grabbing old women like that. If anyone can tell the difference between adolescence and insanity, I'd like to hear it. Come here. Rudy, look at me. What is this about?

RUDY:
Is Heléna in love with that man?

EDDA:
This is why I don't like you calling her that. Sweetheart, you're a perfectly charming young man; you just need to find someone your own age.

RUDY:
What's age got to do with it? I'm a man, she's a woman —

EDDA:
You're a boy.

RUDY:
It's not as if she's made of some rarified substance.

We're both people.

EDDA:

You're a shopkeeper's son, Rudy. You're a Jewish shopkeeper's son. I'm not saying that's a bad thing. But it's a thing. And the sooner you realize that, the sooner you'll grow up a bit. God knows, maybe you're right. Maybe your generation will change things and we'll all be equal and able to love and be loved by whomever we choose. All I know is, little rabbit, right now, we're not. Right now, we have this business to see to. This, what does she call it?

RUDY:

"Déjeuner sur l'herbe." That's French for "lunch on the grass." Considering the spot, we should call it *"Déjeuner sur les mortes."* Lunch on the dead.

EDDA:

(a gravestone) Here's a girl for you. Zdenka Waldner. Nineteen years old and guaranteed not to run away. *(A beat.)* I don't know if Frau Altman is in love with him or not. She's happier than I've seen her in a long time. That's good enough for me.

RUDY:

I don't trust him. I don't like him.

EDDA:

No one asked you.

RUDY:

And you? What about you and Professor Pinchik?

EDDA:

Listen to me, rabbit. Anyone who can turn Mutzi

von Fessendorf's head as you did the other week is going to have no problems in the romance department when the time is right. Until that day, God gave you a right hand for a reason: use it. Here comes Frau Altman. Put out those sandwiches now.

RUDY:
Everyone's found someone but me. It's not fair.

HELÉNA enters, dressed in white.

HELÉNA:
What's not fair? How is everything? Anything we need?

EDDA:
(clasping her hands to her chest) Would you look at that! Ten years younger. I had no recollection of how wonderful you looked in that dress.

HELÉNA:
It's not the dress, Edda, it's this perfect spring blue sky. The world is waking up. Trees are beginning to bud. Rudy, what's happened to your eye? Were you in a fight? Let me look at that.

EDDA:
He was defending his father's good name.

HELÉNA:
I didn't know young men did that anymore. He must be very proud. Did he throw his arms around your neck and kiss you? No, he wouldn't. Tell you what: I shall bestow a kiss upon your wound in his name. Would that be all right?

EDDA:

Don't tease the boy now.

HELÉNA:

Good Sir Knight, kneel and close thine eyes.

> *RUDY kneels and closes his eyes.*

EDDA:

Wonderful. Now you've given him a stiffy.

HELÉNA:

Edda!

EDDA:

He's loving every minute of this.

HELÉNA:

Good Sir Knight, receive this kiss in honor of thy gallant bravery.

> *HELÉNA leans down to kiss his eyelid. RUDY tilts his head and steals a kiss on the lips. HELÉNA pulls away. She tries to give him a smile as though to say, "it's all right," but finds it difficult and turns away.*

RUDY:

Sorry. *(A beat.)* I'm sorry. I'm stupid. I'm — I love you. *(A beat.)* Nobody ever — No one understands. When you look at me, you really see me. You make me someone.

EDDA:

(after a beat; going to him) All right there, Sir Knight. Sir Someone. Arise. If you can. *(As he does, handing him a coin)* Here. That's a good boy. Off you go now.

RUDY:

(a beat) I'm sorry. *(Exiting)* I'm so stupid.

HELÉNA:

(turning) No, Rudy, don't. You're not — *(but he's gone.)*

EDDA:

Shall I open the wine?

HELÉNA:

Only if you'll have a glass with me.

EDDA:

(proceeding to open the wine) I'm no fool.

HELÉNA:

What are these? Edda, you made those little cheese and caviar sandwiches the way I always loved — Oh, these send me right back!

EDDA:

If Hoyos is going to pay the bill, you may as well have some fun. Though I still say, you should have gone to the Prater. Or at least the City Park. What man wants to make love to his lady friend on her dead husband's memorial? *(Handing her a glass of wine)* You're not listening to me, are you?

HELÉNA:

Edda, how long does it take to truly know someone?

EDDA:

(bites into a sandwich, chews, thinks, swallows) Five minutes.

HELÉNA:

What? Stop making jokes.

EDDA:

The only thing you can really know about anyone is, are they kind? Now, given you're smart enough, one can generally figure that out in five minutes. Everything else is likes or dislikes (which change with fashion), or events (what will happen), and those, unless you're clairvoyant, no one can ever know.

HELÉNA:

He's terrible with money. I mean, look at all this! He's going into debt because of me.

EDDA:

You're not married to him. Not your problem.

BÉLA:

(off; singing from Lehar's 'The Merry Widow")
"Lippen schweigen, 's flüstern Geigen: 'Hab mich lieb.'"

HELÉNA:

(singing in response)
"All die Schritte sagen: 'Bitte, hab mich lieb!"

> BÉLA enters. They sing the rest of the verse together, half giggling, half intent.

BÉLA & HELÉNA:

(singing)
"Jeder Druck der Hände deutlich mir 's beschrieb.
Er sagt: 'Klar, 's ist wahr, 's ist wahr. Du hast mich lieb!'"

> HELÉNA and BÉLA laugh and bow as EDDA applauds.

BÉLA:

If my journalist comrades at the *Arbeiter Zeitung* heard

me singing that — ! My whole life I've mocked the Mitteleuropean sentimentality of operetta and now I find I can't get those tunes out of my skull!

EDDA:

Early senility.

BÉLA:

Servus[1], Edda. What's all this? Someone having a party?

HELÉNA:

Don't even pretend to be surprised. I'm shocked you're capable of such bourgeois decadence.

BÉLA:

The best things in life are meant to be free.

EDDA:

(handing him) Here's the bill.

BÉLA:

(pockets it.) How is my Merry Widow? Looking ravishing in white.

> BÉLA and HELÉNA *stare at each other, wanting to kiss, but unwilling to do so in front of Edda.*

HELÉNA:

Shall we... eat?

BÉLA:

I'm ravenous!

EDDA:

Right. I'll be going. Unless, of course —

---

1. A greeting, like the Italian "ciao".

HELÉNA:

No, go! I mean, thank you, Edda. Take a sandwich for the walk.

EDDA:

One was enough, thanks. I'm taking the Professor to a *Heuriger*[1] for blood sausage and wine. Behave yourselves, you two. Bye-bye!

> *EDDA exits. BÉLA stands, watching her go, as HELÉNA prepares a plate for him.*

HELÉNA:

She's developing quite the situation with her Professor Pinchik. Refuses to discuss it which means it must be serious. I'm preparing you a plate. Women are such hypocrites: we see a handsome man and gossip shamelessly; he flirts with us and we'll tell all the town; but the minute it turns serious: *schtum*.[2]

BÉLA:

(quickly going to her) Shut up.

HELÉNA:

Exactly. What?

BÉLA:

She's gone.

> *They kiss, then stare at each other, and loll in each other's arms.*

So whom have you been telling about us?

---

1. a tavern where local winemakers serve their new wine
2. "silent."

HELÉNA:
Me? No one. What is there to tell?

BÉLA:
Must be quite serious then.

HELÉNA:
Béla, there's something I've been wondering. As a journalist, you have friends in — well, in high places. Diplomatic circles, the war archive. Do you know anyone at the police hospital? Only there's a woman was taken there. I've known her all my life. She has a little girl. I don't want her to know it's me. I just want to help. In some way.

BÉLA:
What's her name?

HELÉNA:
(A beat.) Lotte Grunwald.

BÉLA:
I'll find out what I can. I promise.

HELÉNA:
(watching Béla eat) Do you know the tip of your nose moves when you chew? Tell me something you wrote today.

BÉLA:
Something I wrote. A couple in Rudolfsheim were leaving their second floor apartment last week when they dropped to their deaths. Seems they hadn't paid the rent and the landlord had the stairs removed.

HELÉNA:

(laughing) That's horrible! Why am I laughing? I have nightmares about my landlord.

BÉLA:

Oldest definition of comedy: tragedy that happens to someone else.

HELÉNA:

Oh but a tragedy that happens to one's self is so much funnier! Look at me. Look at all of us. We were an empire who thought we could have whatever we wanted whenever we wanted it. So what if we started a war to prove the point? We are the victims! It is our pain that counts! No one sees our sacrifice!

BÉLA:

You have an odd conception of comedy.

HELÉNA:

Being with you does something to me. I feel these rushes of anger. I don't know what to do with them. Anger at Stefan's death; anger at the war; anger our leaders believed their business concerns were worth our lives. Mostly it's anger at myself for being silent, compliant, for watching life go by and things get worse, and doing nothing.

BÉLA:

(kissing her) I really make you happy?

HELÉNA:

Are you asking as a Socialist or a Hungarian?
Yes — ! To a rather frightening degree, if you must know.

BÉLA:

Then will you finally tell me why, of all *gemütlich*[1] places in our *gemütlich* city, you would choose this for our little —

HELÉNA:

Déjeuner sur l'herbe. I'm disappointed, Béla. I thought you of all people would understand. I'm here to say good-bye.

BÉLA:

Good-bye? To me?

HELÉNA:

To him. To this! To Sophie and Zdenka and all things dead and dying. You were right: if I don't embrace life, it'll go on without me. I wanted to be here with you to — to — what's the word? *(Staring at the memorial)* I remember the day Stefan went to war. "I'll see you when all this is over," he said. I'm never coming back here, Béla. It's all finally over.

> *BÉLA holds HELÉNA to him, protecting her. After a silent moment, the sound of an automobile approaching, coming to a stop.*

BÉLA:

We have company.

> *The car honks its horn. They look off.*

HELÉNA:

Oh this is ridiculous. What is she doing here?

> *A silent moment as they stare off at the car.*

---

1. "pleasant and cheerful"

BÉLA:

Is she just going to sit in her Mercedes?

HELÉNA:

Well, it was a nice picnic while it lasted.

BÉLA:

No. I'm not going to let her spoil this. You stay here.

HELÉNA:

Béla, no. You don't know what she's like.

> *The sound of the car door opening, shutting.*

BÉLA:

She's getting out of her car.

HELÉNA:

I had a feeling this might happen. To her, revenge is a work of art.

BÉLA:

Do we wave? Do we smile? What do we do?

HELÉNA:

(packing) Only way to stop her is with a stake through her heart.

> *BÉLA pulls HELÉNA to him and kisses her as MUTZI enters. She stops and looks away.*

(sotto, to Béla) That wasn't wise.

BÉLA:

Frau Fessendorf, what a surprise!

MUTZI:

Apparently. *(A beat.)* I was hoping I would find you

here, Heléna. Though, truth be told, I'd rather you were alone.

BÉLA:

I'll bet.

MUTZI:

This doesn't concern you, Herr Hoyos. As a matter of fact, considering the circumstances, it might be better if you left.

BÉLA:

Frau Fessendorf, as you can see, you've caught us in the middle of lunch. Now the Socialist in me would ask you to join us. However, the Hungarian in me wants to tell you to get back into your car and —

HELÉNA:

(sotto, to Béla) Don't. *(To Mutzi)* He won't say another word.

MUTZI:

(passing through the gate) Perhaps you'd better have a seat and brace yourself. This may come as a shock.

HELÉNA:

(sotto, sitting) This is going to be worse than I thought.

MUTZI:

Heléna, does the name Karl Hupka mean anything to you?

HELÉNA:

For goodness sake, Mutzi! No, the name Karl Hupka means nothing to me. Look, let's not pretend. I know you're angry. I know you're hurt. But please, whatever sordid plan you have going — !

MUTZI:

Karl Hupka was an officer who served alongside your husband at Ypres.

HELÉNA:

Not about Stefan. This is his memorial!

MUTZI:

I'm not the one having lunch on it.

> *MUTZI waves in the direction of the car, motioning to approach.*

HELÉNA:

Who are you waving to?

BÉLA:

There's someone in that car.

MUTZI:

I want you to prepare yourself, Heléna. Good news can be as harrowing as bad. You must be strong.

> *HELÉNA takes BÉLA's hand.*

BÉLA:

Something's wrong here.

MUTZI:

Let go of his hand.

BÉLA:

What?

MUTZI:

Let go of his hand!

The sound of the car door opening and closing.

HELÉNA:

Who is that?

MUTZI:

Hermann was in Holland — in Rotterdam — on diplomatic business. One night, he received a visitor to his room. Like a ghost. Like an answered prayer.

HELÉNA:

What you're doing is wrong. This is wrong.

MUTZI:

He couldn't believe his eyes! Neither could I when they got back night before last. I nearly fainted. The tears of joy! Like a blessing!

HELÉNA:

No!

MUTZI:

Yes! Yes, believe it! For two years, he lived in hiding under the name Karl Hupka, his fallen comrade.

HELÉNA:

They sent me his decoration. They — !

MUTZI:

Hermann tried to explain the danger of coming back, but he refused to listen. All his thoughts, all his hopes have been for you, his loving, faithful wife. For you, Heléna — ! Stefan has come home!

KARL HUPKA (Stefan) enters slowly and cautiously, with a limp and a walking stick. He is older than his years. He is a beaten man.

ACT THREE

The front room of Heléna Altman's apartment as in Act One, but something is noticeably different.

SCENE ONE

Two days later. Late afternoon.

The ticking of a clock. The heavy curtain is pulled back and sun shines through the dirty window onto Rudy's flower, which is now in full bloom. The bedroom door is closed, as is the curtain to the kitchen. Dishes, platters, and various objects packed and awaiting packing in wooden crates. Stacks of newspapers for wrapping. HELÉNA, no longer wearing white, sits lost in thought, an empty glass dangling precariously in her hand. For the past few days, she has walked around in a state of shock.

After a long moment of stillness, the sound of the tea kettle whistling from the kitchen snaps HELÉNA back into action. As the whistle dies, she wraps the glass in newspaper and packs it in a crate. She continues packing.

EDDA pushes open the curtain and enters from the kitchen with two cups of tea. She places them on the table and exits into the kitchen once more. HELÉNA takes up one of the cups of tea and goes to the bedroom door. She knocks quietly and exits, closing the door after her.

EDDA re-emerges from the kitchen, carrying her own cup of tea. She places it next to the other cup, removes the bottle of schnapps from the cabinet and empties it into the two tea cups. She slurps a sip of tea and takes Heléna's place, wrapping and packing. HELÉNA re-enters from the bedroom. She takes up her cup of tea. Sees the empty bottle. The two women exchange a look which seems to say, "What's the point of hiding it anymore?" HELÉNA sits, stirs, and sips as EDDA packs.

EDDA:

(motioning toward the bedroom) Has he slept yet? *(HELÉNA shakes her head.)* Still just sitting there? *(Pause. She continues to pack.)* Oh! I stopped by the Christian Women's League. This gossipy little bureaucrat, ugly as Krampus, told me they can marshal a horse cart at an hour's notice and they'll be happy to take whatever you haven't sold. I told her it wouldn't be enough to fill a whole cart, but apparently it doesn't matter: whether it's a footstool or the contents of the Schönbrunn Palace, they send the same dirty cart. I don't see why you don't ship what's left to yourself in Holland. I know he doesn't want to arouse suspicions, but why on earth, after two years, would anyone care? *(Silence. She looks around.)* I was starting to get used to this place. No matter. No point getting attached to things. You're going to have an adventure. Professor Pinchik tells me Rotterdam has one of the tallest buildings in

all Europe. I can't imagine why that's necessary, but I suppose it's interesting. And no, I haven't told the Professor anything. I haven't told a human soul he's taking you away.

> *HELÉNA looks at her and watches as EDDA packs in silence.*

It's a miracle he's back. A miracle. Took his sweet time. After everything he put you through, after he — *(She changes her mind.)* We don't know what goes on. What men do in war. What war does to men. Still, I never took him for a deserter. There's less of him than I remembered. He used to be — what's the word? He'd walk into a room and... I remember how you two used to laugh; used to come home at all hours and I'd make you both cups of... Now he's sitting in there and tomorrow will be the last day I'll see you in this life of mine, and there's something wrong about that, something deeply wrong.

> *EDDA crosses her arms, looks away, and is silent. From upstairs, the sound of the bad violinist practicing scales. The two women look at each other. They laugh.*

Shall I go up and — ?

> *EDDA makes a strangling motion. HELÉNA dismisses the thought.*

How could he live two years without writing you a letter, without any word at all? Eight months in hospital under an assumed name and then a new life in Holland — Yes, I will speak! Men think the minute they leave the room, the world stops turning and we women hang suspended like coats on a hook, waiting to be taken down. It is only they who suffer the indignities of life's progressions. Or is it war? If war can make a man forget his wife, what is the point of it? What do we care for? Nothing!

> *The violin scale from upstairs has stopped.*

How can such a beautiful world be such a stupid place? It'll all end badly, that's for certain. Last night the Professor took me to the moving pictures. What was it called — ? There was a somnambulist who could see the future. A young man asks him, "If you can tell the future, how long will I live?" The somnambulist opens his terrible eyes: "By dawn tomorrow, you will be dead." Had me scared out of my wits. "The Cabinet of Dr." something — that's what it — "Caligari"!

HELÉNA:
And did he die? The young man.

EDDA:
Stabbed in the throat. I couldn't look. The Professor had to tell me. With you leaving tomorrow, I feel a bit like that young man on his final night. Dreading the icy inevitable hand of fate.

> *The doorbell rings.*

HELÉNA:
Maybe that's your somnambulist now. Answer the door, will you?

EDDA:

(rising to answer the door) I'm not going to miss you one bit.

> *EDDA opens the door a crack.*

BÉLA:

(off) Servus, Edda. Is Frau Altman at home?

EDDA:

I'm sorry, Herr Hoyos; not to you.

BÉLA:

(off) I only want to —

EDDA:

You can't come in.

BÉLA:

(off) Could I leave a note at least?

EDDA:

Certainly; if you have one ready written, I'll see she gets it.

BÉLA:

(off) Have you a pencil I might use?

EDDA:

And you call yourself a journalist.

> *EDDA shuts the door. The violin upstairs plays arpeggios.*

I should get dinner started. I'm making Captain Altman's favorite. If my Tafelspitz doesn't make him realize what he's losing in me, there's no —

> *EDDA is about to clear the table when HELÉNA*

throws her arms around her waist. Pause.

HELÉNA:
God heard my prayers, Edda. He's alive. God heard my prayers and sent my Stefan back to me. Look at me. I'm happy.

EDDA:
I know, my darling. Sometimes we need to speak things to test out if they're true or not.

HELÉNA:
I'm tired is all. Once more I have to uproot my life. Do you think it's possible to love more than one person at a time?

EDDA:
Sadly, no. Or do you mean orgies? I've heard about those. *(With a shake of the head)* Too many choices.

HELÉNA:
What am I ever going to do without you?

EDDA:
A lot of mistakes, I shouldn't wonder.

> *The arpeggios upstairs stop. The doorbell rings.*

For the love of God! *(Opening and slamming the door)* I said, "No!"

> *Seeing that she has slammed the door on a smiling MUTZI, EDDA freezes in her tracks.*

HELÉNA:
(a fierce whisper) Into the kitchen! Into the kitchen!

> *Utterly disgraced, EDDA exits into the kitchen.*

> HELÉNA *steps toward the door and waits. After a pause, there is a slow knock from without.* HELÉNA *opens the door cheerfully.*

Mutzi, what a surprise!

MUTZI:

Did Edda just — ?

HELÉNA:

Do come in. You've caught us in the middle of packing. *(Kisses her cheeks.)* Will you take some tea? *(Calling)* Edda, tea! Is it stuffy in here? I'd open that window only I'm afraid it's painted shut.

MUTZI:

Has Edda gone red? Has she become one of those Socialists? What is going on here? Heléna, have you been drinking?

HELÉNA:

(quickly breathes into her hand and smells it) No, you can't smell it.

MUTZI:

Where's Stefan?

HELÉNA:

Dead, didn't you know?

> MUTZI *regards her, but decides to rise above her childishness. She produces papers.*

MUTZI:

I came to bring your train tickets and custom forms.

HELÉNA:
My, but you think of everything.

MUTZI:
We were going to book you into First, but Hermann pointed out, what if someone were to recognize Stefan on board, which I thought very smart of him. I'm seeing a whole new side of Hermann because of this. It's rather marvelous to realize one's husband has a brain after all. He says Third Class offers the best chance of anonymity, so that's what we went with. And you're to change trains at Wiesbaden. You'll be traveling as Herr and Frau Hupka, of course.

HELÉNA:
What's my Christian name?

MUTZI:
Your what?

HELÉNA:
You have my future pretty well laid out. I was wondering if I'm to have a new name as well. What goes with Hupka?

MUTZI:
You mustn't scoff at precautions.

HELÉNA:
Heidi?

> *The tea kettle whistles, off.*

MUTZI:
I hear wonderful things about Rotterdam. The sea air is supposed to be very —

HELÉNA:

Bernard. That's it: Bernard Hupka. I'll grow a goatee and wear a monocle and say, "indubitably!"

MUTZI:

Will you stop it? I always knew you were an angry woman.

HELÉNA:

Mutzi, you have no idea.

MUTZI:

These fantasies you concoct in your head: everyone's always against you. Show me a single soul who has been a better friend to you.

HELÉNA:

It's true. You're a saint. We should write the Pope.

MUTZI:

Enough! Where is Stefan? I come over and you're not even in the same room with him, and you're drunk!

HELÉNA:

You were always like that. Even when we were girls: Lotte was the joker, I was the dreamer, and you were the one in control. But Lotte knew how to make you laugh. Or is that something you choose not to remember? After all, she's nothing but a whore.

MUTZI:

She's dead.

> *EDDA enters, carrying the tea tray, extremely drunk. She deposits the tray on the table before Mutzi, turns*

and exits. MUTZI waits till she's out of earshot.

It was in the papers yesterday. The city is covering her burial fees, thanks to their Socialistic 'bleed the rich' tax program. Which basically means I'm paying for it. Whatever happened to facing the consequences of one's actions?

HELÉNA:

How can you not care?

MUTZI:

Me? If my husband had been gone two years, I can tell you, I'd be at his side every moment of his return. What kind of wife are you?

HELÉNA:

No! You have no idea what goes on in my marriage. *(She starts pouring the tea.)*

MUTZI:

She's a drunk, he's a deserter, how good a marriage could it be?

> *HELÉNA continues pouring hot tea beyond the cups in Mutzi's direction, MUTZI cries out and leaps from her chair. They are still, staring at each other.*

I should go.

HELÉNA:

Won't you stay for tea?

> *The bedroom door opens and KARL appears, without his walking stick.*

KARL:

Heléna — Ah, Countess von Fessendorf, forgive me.

(Offers a small stiff bow.)

MUTZI:

Not at all, Captain Altman.

HELÉNA:

What is it, my darling?

KARL:

Nothing that can't wait.

MUTZI:

Please, I was just on my way out. I only came by to drop off your traveling papers. *(Offering Stefan her hand)* Sadly, Captain, I don't believe we shall meet again. Life has these little curves: one turns a corner and loses sight of people. Even those who once were so close. I'd like to think we'll all meet up again somehow but... *Qui vivra, verra. C'est malheureux, mais c'est comme ça!*[1] Safe journey tomorrow, Captain.

> *Having overheard, EDDA has wandered on from the kitchen. KARL kisses Mutzi's hand.*

KARL:

Please thank your husband for all he has done. I account you both true friends.

> *MUTZI goes to the door. She waits for Edda to open the door. EDDA doesn't move. Awkwardly, MUTZI negotiates the doorknob and exits.*

HELÉNA:

What is it, Stefan?

---

1. "Time will tell. It's unfortunate, but that's how it is!"

KARL:

My old gramophone machine, where is it? *(Pause. Off her look)* It occurred to me we might put on a record and you and I might dance.

HELÉNA:

...Dance? But your leg —

KARL:

You used to like dancing. Or am I wrong? I used to like watching you dance.

EDDA:

The gramophone's been sold, Herr Altman. Quite some time ago.

KARL:

Sold? You sold my — ? *(A beat.)* Of course.

> *HELÉNA doesn't move. KARL considers returning to the bedroom.*

Do you recall our last dance together, Heléna? I do. The Officers' Farewell. It was ladies' choice. You wore the pearl brooch my mother'd given you. And you kept smiling for my sake so that I wouldn't see you sad. There was champagne and confetti and we all sang songs and... I remember it well. We were marvelous.

EDDA:

Wait — Captain Altman, don't you move! Frau Altman, a minute — I'll be right back!

> *EDDA rushes out of the apartment. Pause.*

KARL:

Do you know what she's — ?

>   *HELÉNA shakes her head and shrugs. Pause.*

I could hum.

HELÉNA:
You could — ?

KARL:
Hum.

>   *STEFAN hums "Tales from the Vienna Woods." He approaches her slowly.*

HELÉNA:
How many times did I dream of this? Don't do this. Please.

KARL:
(drawing very close) Shhh! I'm here now.

HELÉNA:
You can't simply —

KARL:
I'm here now.

>   *He takes her in his arms just as, from upstairs, the violin begins playing "Tales from the Vienna Woods." They dance. It is slow and awkward with his limp, but shows exquisite style.*

You were bickering, weren't you? With Mutzi. Over some silliness, I shouldn't wonder. I've missed my little Lenchen's[1] charming silliness. I'm glad to be taking her away from arguments and creditors and this ugly apartment. You'll see. You'll have a whole new set of friends to have tea and bicker with.

---

1. "Lenchen" is a German diminutive for Heléna.

You'll never have another worry. I'll see to it.

> *HELÉNA has been laughing. She slows her dancing and stops. She kisses Karl. Her passion grows, along with his awkwardness. He tries to put an end to this intimacy, but she begins undoing his trousers. He pulls away.*

What are you doing?

HELÉNA:

Don't you want to see how I paid the bills? Don't you want to know what your wife did?

> *Silence. KARL exits, shaking his head.*

> *EDDA enters, smiling and expectant, only to find HELÉNA alone.*

SCENE TWO

The next day. Early afternoon.

All major furniture is gone, or in the process of being removed by workmen, along with the stacks of wooden crates. EDDA, hammer in hand, is overseeing the removal. All that will remain are a simple wooden chair, a small ugly end table, and Rudy's flower on the window.

EDDA:
(following the workmen out the door) Careful with that, it's got dishes! How do you say it in — Badz ostrożny!¹ *(To herself)* What beer hall did they drag him out of?

BÉLA:
(entering) "Nymph, in thy orisons be all my sins remembered."

EDDA:
No! Out! Herr Hoyos, you're not to be here. Not today of all days.

BÉLA:
(taking her in his arms) But I can't go on without you another minute, Edda!

---
1. "Be careful!"

EDDA:

Then you'll have to suffer or go hang yourself somewhere. And before you ask, Frau Altman's packing her clothes and doesn't need to see you. She put me in charge of these movers from the Christian Women's League and I tell you, they must have had too much wine at mass or something.

BÉLA:

They're Poles. They're born drunk. But tell me, where is... Herr Hupka?

EDDA:

Herr Hupka isn't feeling well. Truth is, he thought it better to keep a low profile while the movers were here. You understand.

BÉLA:

Is he still afraid someone's going to — ? No one gives a damn he deserted, not anymore. With the reds in power, he might even get congratulated. But he'd rather skulk off to live in exile in the Netherlands like Kaiser Wilhelm. It's self-pity like that which started the whole mess.

EDDA:

I thought the Serbs started it at Sarajevo.

BÉLA:

Sarajevo was an assassination. A horrible thing. But when you answer a horrible thing with an even more horrible thing, you have begun a morally corrupt conversation. You see this coin? Get Frau Altman to come in here and leave us alone to talk and it's yours.

EDDA:

She doesn't want to see you.

BÉLA:

I'm counting on your greed to convince her otherwise.

EDDA:

(*pause. Taking the coin*) I don't need your money but I'll keep it. Professor Pinchik has hired me on as his housekeeper.

BÉLA:

Is that what you're calling it?

EDDA:

Watch it.

BÉLA:

Going to iron thewrinkles out of his linens, are you?

> *BÉLA kisses her cheek. EDDA puts down the hammer and heads to the door. Knocks quietly.*

HELÉNA:

(*off*) Yes? (*Pause.*) What is it?

EDDA:

Could you come out here a moment please?

> *EDDA motions for BÉLA to move out of the direct line of sight of the door. He does. HELÉNA enters, closing the door quietly after her. She turns, sees Béla, stops.*

HELÉNA:

Edda, no. Show him out.

EDDA:

(picking up the last of the crates) I can't at the moment; this has to get on the cart before those drunken Poles drive off.

> *EDDA exits, shutting the door after her. A silence.*

BÉLA:

I came to say a proper good-bye.

HELÉNA:

Good-bye.

BÉLA:

I have news about your friend Lotte. I'm afraid we're too late.

HELÉNA:

I heard.

BÉLA:

They used to call it the French Disease. Far more charming than syphilis. They tried arsenic treatments. In a lucid moment, she got hold of her chart and prescribed herself an overdose.

HELÉNA:

And the child?

BÉLA:

(shaking his head) Lost. There's no record. I'm sorry.

HELÉNA:

I keep thinking, I could have done so much more than a silly basket of food.

BÉLA:

We all could do so much more for each other while

we're alive. People die, suddenly we take notice.

HELÉNA:

Thank you for stopping by. For bringing me the news.

BÉLA:

Wait. Heléna — !

HELÉNA:

My husband is in the next room.

BÉLA:

I wouldn't care if he were on the moon.

HELÉNA:

You're not a stupid man, Béla. Things have changed. When I married Stefan, I took a vow. That comes first. It has to.

BÉLA:

Can you not show a little sympathy at least? Mutzi's been hunting me like a red stag. Tracking me. Showing up places. Sending me notes: "A broken heart that's kept alone will fester; call on me, rely on me, depend on me."

HELÉNA:

All this in two days?

BÉLA:

She's a witch. She sold her soul to the Devil to raise your husband from the dead.

HELÉNA:

That isn't funny.

BÉLA:

A gypsy says to a woman, "I can look into the

seeds of time, and see that your husband will die a violent and horrible death." "Oh my God," says the woman, "will I be acquitted?"

HELÉNA:

You need to go now.

BÉLA:

That was funny.

HELÉNA:

I'm pleased you think so.

BÉLA:

I'm only trying to laugh because it's all so miserable.

HELÉNA:

(*offering a handshake*) Allow me to wish you well.

BÉLA:

You can't go. I'll hold you captive. I'll tie you by the waist to the Anchor Clock and every hour it chimes, we'll dance around the market square. We'll become the local eccentrics. Stories will circulate. Neighborhood children will watch us grow old. When we die (which will be together, smiling in each other's arms), the city of Vienna will weep. I told you I talk too much.

HELÉNA:

It's a beautiful fantasy, Béla. In another life, perhaps. I'm sorry.

BÉLA:

What if I were to die? Of a broken heart. It happens. Leave him. Run away with me. You're not the same as when I met you. You've blossomed. If only I knew you were happy to be going. If you can tell me that — and I don't believe you are — but if you can say it —

HELÉNA:
I am.

BÉLA:
(a beat) You are.

HELÉNA:
I don't know. I've no idea what I am anymore. But I do, at long last, understand what a marriage is. It's a structure which guides us when we're lost. When we don't know where to turn, it tells us what we can or cannot do.

BÉLA:
What a draconian concept.

HELÉNA:
Béla, you woke me from a deep sleep. I'm still blinking. And I'm grateful. But we've known each other, what, two, three months? That's no basis for anything. What kind of existence would it be if we were slaves to every passing whim? That's the life of a mad person.

BÉLA:
I shouldn't have asked if you're happy; I should have asked if you even want to be.

HELÉNA:
Of course I — look, perhaps it's best if you go.

BÉLA:
(*advancing on her*) I don't believe you.

HELÉNA:
What?

BÉLA:
Look me in the eye.

HELÉNA:
Why are you — Please, don't stand so close.

BÉLA:
Look me in the eye.

HELÉNA:
Béla, my husband's —

BÉLA:
It's very simple. Just look me in the eye and —

> HELÉNA *grabs Béla and kisses him. Desperately. Passionately. He backs her against the wall and raises her skirts.*

HELÉNA:
We can't!

BÉLA:
We can.

HELÉNA:
We have to stop.

BÉLA:
Shhh.

HELÉNA:
This is madness!

BÉLA:

Quiet. Quietly. Quietly.

> *They begin to make love. She stares into his eyes and weeps. She pulls him to her and holds him. It becomes too much.*

HELÉNA:

No — No — You have to stop — Béla — !

> *She pushes him away roughly as the door to the bedroom opens and KARL appears. BÉLA turns away as he does up his trousers. HELÉNA is quick to dry her eyes as she pretends to be crying from laughter.*

Stop it, you're making me cry with laughter! Oh, Stefan, you must hear this! Béla was telling the funniest story. Apparently a gypsy who can tell the future says to this woman — how does it go? —

BÉLA:

"Your husband will die a violent and horrible death."

HELÉNA:

Yes, that's right, and the woman says —

KARL:

"Will I be acquitted?"

HELÉNA:

(a beat) Oh.

KARL:

Have the movers gone? We ought to be getting ready.

HELÉNA:

Yes, Edda saw them out. Darling, you remember Béla Hoyos.

BÉLA:

(*offering his hand*) Good to see you again, Captain.

KARL:

(*ignoring him*) You know, without the distraction of furniture, one gets a shockingly clear view of how ugly this apartment truly is.

HELÉNA:

Oh?

BÉLA:

Will you not shake my hand?

HELÉNA:

I've yet to be able to afford an opinion about it, myself.

KARL:

Oh yes. If this sordid little flat were a human being, it would be a hunchbacked Hungarian onion-seller. Or a journalist for one of the socialist papers.

BÉLA:

Now that's funny.

KARL:

(*to Béla*) Why are you here?

HELÉNA:

Now Stefan, Béla merely came to say good-bye.

KARL:

Good-bye.

BÉLA:

(to Heléna) Ah, the vernacular of a married couple. You're very much his wife.

KARL:

I'm glad you've taken notice of that.

BÉLA:

I could say the same to you, Odysseus; now you're back from the Land of the Lotus Eaters.

HELÉNA:

(laughing) Why do I feel as though I'm in a comedy by Beaumarchais?

KARL:

Because Beaumarchais wrote about adultery. *(to Béla)* Now that's funny.

BÉLA:

Judging by the way you're glaring at me, Captain, I'd say we ought to be standing on a steep mountain face, about to lock horns.

KARL:

Thanks in no small measure to the cuckold's horns with which she has crowned me, and the smirking way you call me Captain. Tell me, Hoyos, how exactly did you meet Heléna?

HELÉNA:

Wonderful — we're behaving like children.

KARL:

I am exercising my right as your husband by having a civilized conversation with this man.

HELÉNA:
That's very charming but we ought to go. We have a train to catch.

BÉLA:
You speak of a husband's rights, Captain, yet show little understanding of his responsibilities. Of course, I know nothing of either, never having married.

KARL:
How much did she charge you? You are one of her customers? Or does she prefer the term 'client'?

BÉLA:
Mutzi von Fessendorf introduced us, if you must know.

KARL:
(*a wry laugh*) Do you honestly expect me to stand here and believe yours is a respectable friendship?

BÉLA:
Not at all, Captain; you can stand wherever you like.

KARL:
What kind of fool do you take me for?

BÉLA:
What are my choices?

HELÉNA:
All right. Are we done?

KARL:
Don't insult my intelligence, Hoyos. I know you've had carnal relations with my wife. What was that

when I came in a moment ago, a game of tag? She's a whore. You suddenly seem rather lachrymose. No witty rejoinder? My God, I know that look. We had a term for it during the war. Hupka came up with it. You see, we had these cheap French tarts a few miles from the front lines —

HELÉNA:

(turning to go) This is ridiculous —

KARL:

Be still! Some of the men, some of them were so starved for affection, they'd create wild romantic notions about these toothless hags. Fantasies these sluts were really misunderstood victims of circumstance; deep down they were good daughters, sisters, mothers; they could be saved with love! Cunt-struck, that's what we called the poor devils. Or cunt-blind. As I believe you are.

BÉLA:

All this must have been before you deserted your men in battle.

KARL stares at Béla. Silence.

KARL:

What were you? I always had a knack for guessing. I'd say a stretcher carrier. You have the look of someone who couldn't bring himself to fire a gun.

HELÉNA:

You're wrong. Béla fought. Didn't you? Tell him.

KARL:

Or are you one of those pacifists who don't believe

in war?

BÉLA:

You have the nerve to say that after running away —

KARL:

You don't need to recite my accomplishments. I know what I did.

HELÉNA:

Béla saw his share of battle. Tell him.

KARL:

Certainly he saw it. From a safe remove. What was it, a field hospital? Lots of pretty nurses?

BÉLA:

I worked in the War Archive. Cataloging propaganda.

HELÉNA:

What? But you said — you told me —

BÉLA:

I've never fired a gun. Or even held one. I find it immoral. I'm sorry if I made you believe otherwise.

KARL:

One learned to tell who'd been to the front and who hadn't. You lose something out there. You come back less. Yet carrying something more. Something you didn't want but can't get rid of. Like a stink. Why am I telling you? I witnessed better men than you mown down like wheat. I know you've had my wife. What am I supposed to do about that?

BÉLA:

Be grateful for her.

> *KARL punches BÉLA in the face. BÉLA falls. HELÉNA rushes to Béla's aid.*

It's all right. I'm fine.

HELÉNA:

Are you proud of yourself? Barbaric!

KARL:

He's fine! He said he's fine! See, the sun is shining: everything's fine! Let's open a bottle; I'll drink his health.

HELÉNA:

(helping Béla stand) You'll need some ice on that and I haven't any.

KARL:

Stop coddling him! I've never known such a maternal instinct in a barren woman. Go see if there's anything in the kitchen. Maybe some kirsch. Edda was always forgetful.

HELÉNA:

It's probably best we say good-bye now. Please allow me to apologize on behalf of my husband —

KARL:

Don't you dare.

HELÉNA:

It's been a distinct pleasure knowing you. I will always think kindly of you. Be happy. You deserve to be.

BÉLA:

And you?

KARL:

Get out.

BÉLA:

(A pause. He kisses her hand) Enchanté, Madam. You will always be my Niobe. *(A beat.)* Captain.

> *BÉLA exits. Pause.*

KARL:

See if there's a bottle in the kitchen, will you?

HELÉNA:

Is this what it's to be? Is this our future? Humiliating me with these theatrics? Making me pay? Anytime I talk to a man… How dare you strike him? Have you any idea how dear he was to me?

> *Silence.*

KARL:

I didn't come back for this.

> *Silence.*

HELÉNA:

I don't know how to talk to you anymore.

KARL:

I heard you from the next room. Not what you were saying but how you said it. Your tone. You sounded… Then seeing how you looked at him. You're an officer's wife, for God's sake. I don't expect things to be as they were, Heléna, but —

He takes her hand.

Heléna, what do you say when we get on that train today, it'll be as though the past never happened? We wipe the slate clean and start afresh. The war, this apartment, this life you led — leave them behind. Put them from your mind. Imagine I'd only gone out to the corner for a newspaper and I'm back. We'll never be apart again.

HELÉNA:

Assuming all that were possible, Stefan, how would we do that?

KARL:

It's so simple. I see it now. Once I look beyond my emotions and stubborn reactions. It's here in the room with us. Heléna, more than anything, I want to be able to touch you again. To hold you to me without feeling rage. Without seeing you looking at him. And I can. Everything is very clear now, as though I just woke up. *(A beat.)* I forgive you, Heléna. *(Off her look)* See? Isn't it wonderful? I forgive you! You didn't know what you were doing. Overwhelmed by grief, feeling abandoned — it's no wonder you wanted to hurt me. Who's to say what I would have done in your shoes but lose myself in pleasure? Sex and death. I understand. You were always so easily led. Give me your hands. Shhh. I'm going to make it all right. I forgive you. Clean slate. Now let's see if I can find a bottle of something and we'll toast our new life together.

KARL kisses her on the forehead and exits into the kitchen, humming "Tales From the Vienna Woods."

(*off*) We've plenty of time to make the train. Wait till you see Rotterdam. Might take some getting used to at first, but — Ah, here we are: schnapps!

> *HELÉNA takes up the hammer. KARL re-enters with a bottle. HELÉNA swings at him savagely, but misses. Grabbing the table or the chair, he puts himself on other side of it, protectively. Grunting, she swings again. He ducks back.*
>
> *A standoff.*
>
> *Hesitatingly at first, KARL goes to the door. He collects his coat. Checks the travel papers in the breast pocket. He looks back at Heléna. He exits, leaving the door ajar.*
>
> *Spent, HELÉNA's arm drops to her side, the hammer from her hand. For a moment, she remains still, dazed and in shock.*
>
> *Silence.*
>
> *She goes to the window. Tries opening it. It's painted shut. A timid knock and EDDA appears in the doorway..*

EDDA:

(*knocking*) Frau Altman...? (*Knocks again.*)

> *EDDA sees Heléna and enters slowly, cautiously.*

Hadn't you better — ? I saw Captain Altman come storming through the front door. Went clear up the street.

EDDA sees the hammer on the floor. She looks to Heléna. She understands that something violent has happened.

What's happened here?... Are you hurt?

But HELÉNA doesn't respond.

You can tell me if he hurt you.

HELÉNA:
(pause. distant) No. No, Edda, I'm fine.

EDDA:
What about your train? Aren't you going to miss your train?

HELÉNA:
...Yes...Yes, I imagine I am.

Silence.

EDDA:
He found out, didn't he?

HELÉNA looks at her. Silence.

HELÉNA:
...I'm going to stay.

EDDA:
Stay?

HELÉNA nods.

But Frau Altman, everything's gone. How are you to — ?

Pause. EDDA looks around.

Is there anyone I can — Shall I send for Herr

121

Hoyos? Oh but I'm sure he'd be pleased to help. Why, he could —

HELÉNA:
...No. No, Edda. That's over with.

EDDA:
What?

HELÉNA:
That's done.

EDDA:
I don't understand.

> *HELÉNA goes to the window and looks out.*

HELÉNA:
Look how green the trees. It'll be summer before we know it. *(Notices and takes up Rudy's flower. She takes it slowly from the sill to the table.)* I should take Rudy's flower out somewhere nice and plant it. Out among other living things. Would be good to feel my hands in the earth. Find something to do. Something that matters.

EDDA:
Frau Altman, is there anything I can do?

> *HELÉNA returns to the window and tries to open it.*

HELÉNA:
I need to —

EDDA:
(exiting into the kitchen) Wait — ! There's a broken blade in the rubbish — you can use it to cut through the old paint —

EDDA disappears into the kitchen.

HELÉNA:
I just need... I need to —

HELÉNA struggles with the window. We hear the paint crack and suddenly it gives way and opens. A spring breeze blows into the room. HELÉNA breathes. Her breathing calms. HELÉNA closes her eyes.

HELÉNA:
...breathe.

End of play.